I'LL HAVE THE
Risotto!

50 delicious recipes for Italian rice dishes

Maxine Clark

RYLAND PETERS & SMALL
LONDON • NEW YORK

Dedication

I dedicate this book to my friend Pia Scavia, a Milanese who is both inspirational and stoic and doesn't mind using a stock cube.

Designers Steve Painter, Toni Kay and Paul Stradling
Editor Kate Eddison
Head of Production Patricia Harrington
Creative Director Leslie Harrington
Editorial Director Julia Charles

Food Stylists Maxine Clark and Bridget Sargeson
Prop Stylist Helen Trent
Indexer Hilary Bird

First published in 2011 with an extended edition published in 2015 & 2018. This edition published in 2024 by Ryland Peters & Small
20–21 Jockey's Fields
London WC1R 4BW
and
341 E 116th St
New York NY 10029
www.rylandpeters.com

10 9 8 7 6 5 4 3 2 1

Notes

• All spoon measurements are level unless otherwise stated.
• Eggs are UK medium/US large unless otherwise specified. Uncooked or partly cooked eggs should not be served to the very old, the frail, young children, pregnant women or those with compromised immune systems.

Author's acknowledgments

My thanks go to all at RPS; Elsa and Alison for encouraging me to write this book and Steve for his patience at the studio, his good design and enthusiastic risotto tasting. Martin produced beautiful, natural-looking photographs with a subject that is difficult to control. Helen supplied evocative props and backgrounds. My thanks to Bridget, for producing some really beautiful risottos. Thanks too must go to Silvia Brugiamolini at Esperya – the rice was a treat to use. I would like to thank Antonietta Kelly at the Italian Trade Commission for supplying information from The Italian Association of Rice Producers. Thanks also go to Nowelle Valentino-Capezza for her help with the translations.

contents

introduction

Making a risotto is one of the most calming, sensuous, satisfying cooking experiences I know. Make it in a hurry at your peril – this is a dish to be made after a hard day, while you're winding down with a glass of wine. Though the cooking process takes only about 30 minutes from beginning to end, it's best to do all the preparation before you start cooking the rice. Have the stock ready and keep it hot over very gentle heat while you make the risotto.

There are no sudden movements when risotto-making. The butter is melted very gently, the chopped vegetables are added and slowly cooked in their own juices until soft. The rice is added and pan-toasted until it smells vaguely nutty, then the wine is splashed in 'with a sigh'. The stock is gently ladled in, sighing again each time. Then the rice is stirred languorously to encourage the starch to leave the outside of the grains and thicken the sauce. The bubbles in the liquid move and burst slowly. The rice should always look voluptuous and never be allowed to dry out.

Almost anything can be cooked into a risotto – and it can be added right at the beginning before the rice if it should be cooked for longer than 12–20 minutes, or it can be stirred in at the end. Traditional methods of cooking vegetable risottos like asparagus involve adding the vegetables early so they disintegrate into the risotto, cooking and sealing the flavour into the creaminess of the dish. It is now more fashionable to stir in precooked vegetables to give a contrast between mild creamy rice and the added ingredient. But it is all a matter of taste. People get very wound up about whether a risotto should be soupy and very firm – others like it creamy and thick. Ignore what people say and cook it as you like it. Just don't overcook it to a mushy porridge – that is unkind to the rice as well as your taste buds.

ingredients and utensils

The cultivation of rice in Italy
The cultivation of rice is as ancient as the making of wine and olive oil, thus providing a staple on which people could survive. Italian rice has its genetic roots in the original species Oryza sativa, a member of the Gramineae or grass family, the japonica subspecies of which is said to have been brought to Europe through Arab expansion into the Mediterranean basin. It was probably known before this time, arriving via the busy trade routes with the Middle and Far East, where it had been cultivated for thousands of years. The japonica has a higher starch content than the

other most important subspecies, indica. Italian rice cultivation is concentrated in the Po Valley in northern Italy (Piedmont and Lombardy), but it is also grown around Venice, in Emilia Romagna, Sardinia and a little in Tuscany and Calabria. Rice production soared in the latter part of the nineteenth century after the development of manageable irrigation in Vercelli in Piedmont coupled with the invention of bigger and better rice-milling machinery. Vercelli is now the epicentre of rice-growing in Europe and has a rice stock exchange, the Borsa del Riso. New varieties have been developed since the singular variety simply called nostrale was consumed across Italy for over 400 years from the fifteenth century, so that more than 50 varieties are now available. Although rice is no longer considered a staple or 'food of the poor', the average Italian still eats about 5 kilograms of rice per year, in the late 19th century, it was more than double that amount.

Rice is planted in flooded fields in March, and takes 180 days to grow and finally ripen for harvest in October. Until 40 years ago, rice was still picked by hand, but now it is gathered by huge combine harvesters. It is reaped, threshed and dried, then sold for milling and distribution. The milling process removes any dust, immature grains and the outer husk. Then it is polished to remove a second 'sheath' and the broken grains removed from the whole ones. Some rice is still polished all'antica (in the old way) using stone pestles (lavorato con pestelli) that give the grain a rougher, more rustic appearance and a little more fibre.

Which Italian risotto rice is best?
There are three varieties readily available around the world: arborio, carnaroli and vialone nano – these are the best for making risotto. In general, I like to use carnaroli or vialone nano, with arborio being last though not least favourite. Arborio is the most popular variety of short grain risotto rice. It has a slightly higher 'stickiness' or starch rating which makes it good for timbales and very creamy risottos. Personally, I think that arborio can become too mushy too quickly, whereas carnaroli has wonderful absorption, releases enough starch to make the risotto creamy and not sticky, while the grains still remain firm – al dente. Carnaroli is the rice preferred by most Italian cooks. Vialone nano has a shorter grain, a good absorption when cooked and is another rice with low stickiness or starch. This is preferred in the Veneto and Mantova in Lombardy for traditional recipes that require a looser risotto with a firm grain. Other newer risotto varieties available in Italy are baldo and Roma,

which are both high in starch and make very creamy risottos and good timbales. There are many other types of rice, but not all are suitable for risotto-making.

Italian rice is divided into four group classifications by law: *originario* or *comune*, *semifino*, *fino* and *superfino*. This doesn't denote quality or 'cookability', but length, appearance and shape. Every packet should display the group and variety.

Can I use another rice instead of Italian risotto rice?

No. Rice suitable for making risotto has a 'pearl' in the centre of the grain. On inspection, you will clearly see that the centre is whiter than the surrounding edges. This opaque central zone is made up of a farinaceous starch that is different from the starch on the outside of the grain. During cooking the outside starch dissolves into the liquid when the rice is stirred or beaten, while the interior starch absorbs liquid and swells. Indica rices such as basmati, Thai jasmine and American long grain rice do not have this 'pearl' in the centre. Therefore, Italian risotto rice is the only rice with the right make-up to absorb a large amount of liquid, release starch as it is stirred to make a creamy sauce, yet retain the shape and firmness of the grain without disintegrating and becoming gluey. Risotto is never gluey – it is always moist and creamy.

How do I store rice?

Rice absorbs moisture and odours, so store it like wine in a cool, dry, airy place. I keep it in an airtight storage jar well away from the oven or stove-top. If you like the look of the packaging, put the whole thing into a glass preserving jar with a rubber seal, close and admire!

What does *al dente* mean?

This means that the centre of the grain of rice is still firm to the bite, but cooked and definitely not mushy. It still has some delicate resistance. Some (especially the Venetians) say that the rice should still be a little gritty or chalky in the centre, but this is personal and I do not like it like that. You can take this al dente business too far.

Butter – salted or unsalted?

Always unsalted – it gives a purer, sweeter flavour.

Real stock or cubes?

Ideally, real stock is better, as it is the heart of the risotto, but it must not be too strong. Realistically, most Italians would use a stock cube to make an everyday risotto, but they are lucky to have quite a choice available and I think that their cubes are of a better quality than those available elsewhere. *Gusto Classico* is a good all-round flavour – it is light and suitable for meat or poultry dishes.

How much stock?

As much as the rice will take. Always have more stock ready than the recipe states – you never know how much that particular rice will absorb on that particular day. It depends on and the type of pan you use and how fast the rice is bubbling (too fast and the stock evaporates instead of being absorbed into the rice).

Which pan to use?

A medium to large shallow pan (but not like a frying pan) with a heavy base. Enamelled cast iron or heavy stainless steel with a sandwiched base are good. I have a deep, heavy-gauge aluminium sauté pan that is perfect for risotto-making. A thin, flimsy pan is not suitable – the rice will stick and burn and you will not be able to control the simmer. Use too wide or shallow a pan, and the stock will evaporate too quickly and concentrate its flavour too much into the rice. Too deep and the rice will take ages to cook – it will stew and become mushy. All in all, a heavy saucepan that is not too deep is the answer. Make sure it is big enough to enable you to stir comfortably and for the rice to swell.

Parmigiano Reggiano or bust!

You do not have to use real Parmigiano Reggiano for risotto all the time. Parmigiano is a hard grana cheese with a D.O.P. status (Denominazione d'Origine Protetta), which promotes the authenticity and artisan characteristics of certain food and agricultural products – this one can come only from the provinces of Modena, Reggio Emilia, Parma and part of Bologna and Mantua, and is made in a particular way. Grana Padano D.O.P. is a less expensive grana cheese made in the Po Valley, and is perfectly acceptable to stir into a risotto. Fresh grana should smell sweet and nutty – never use the stuff found in the round cardboard canister. Extra cheese is not generally served with a fish or seafood risotto, the one exception being black squid ink risotto.

To shave or not to shave …

Personally, I don't like shaved Parmesan on a risotto – it sticks to the rice like a soggy blanket and the heat makes it floppy and greasy. I prefer the cheese finely grated almost to a powder, so it will melt smoothly into the risotto.

SIMPLE RISOTTOS

basic risotto

risotto in bianco

about 1.5 litres/6 cups hot Vegetable Stock (page 149) or Chicken Stock (page 150)

125 g/1 stick unsalted butter

1 onion, finely chopped

500 g/2⅓ cups risotto rice

150 ml/⅔ cup dry white wine (optional)

freshly grated Parmesan (optional)

sea salt and freshly ground black pepper

SERVES 4–6

This is the method for a basic, unflavoured risotto without cheese. The important thing is not to rush making a risotto – treat it with love and respect and you will achieve perfect results. The method always remains the same, but the ingredients change slightly. Sometimes, instead of plain onion, a *soffritto* – a finely chopped mixture of white onion, carrot and celery – can delicately flavour the base of a risotto. Cubed pancetta is sometimes added, but must not be allowed to colour or it will become tough. Although the stated amount of stock is correct, I like to top it up to 2 litres/quarts just in case the rice becomes too thick (you could use hot water instead). Venetians believe risotto should be served *all'onda* (like a wave), referring to its liquid texture – so you may like to add a little more hot stock just before you serve to loosen it, but don't let the risotto wait too long or the rice will turn mushy. This recipe gives 4 generous servings or 6 smaller servings.

making a basic risotto step-by-step

(1) Put the stock in a saucepan and keep at a gentle simmer. Melt half of the butter in a separate large, heavy-based saucepan and add the onion. Cook gently for 10 minutes, until soft, golden and translucent but not browned.

(2) Add the rice to the onions and stir until well coated with the butter and heated through (this is called the *tostatura* and the rice should start to crackle slightly).

(3) Pour in the wine, if using – you should hear a *sospiro* (sigh) as it is added. Boil hard until it has reduced and almost disappeared. This will remove the raw taste of alcohol.

(4) Begin adding the stock, a large ladleful at a time, stirring gently until each ladleful has been almost absorbed into the rice. The risotto should be kept at a bare simmer throughout cooking, so don't let the rice dry out – add more stock as necessary. Continue until the rice is tender and creamy, but the grains still firm. This should take 15–20 minutes, depending on the type of rice used – check the packet instructions.

(5) Taste and season well with salt and pepper and beat in the remaining butter (this process of beating is called *mantecare*). Sometimes grated Parmesan cheese is beaten in with the butter at this stage. Cover and let rest for a couple of minutes then serve.

pesto risotto

risotto al pesto

about 1.5 litres/6 cups hot Vegetable Stock (page 149) and Chicken Stock (page 150)

125 g/1 stick unsalted butter

1 onion, finely chopped

500 g/2⅓ cups risotto rice

150 ml/⅔ cup dry white wine (optional)

1 quantity homemade Pesto Genovese (see page 18) or good-quality freshly prepared pesto

sea salt and freshly ground black pepper

SERVES 6

Stirring homemade pesto genovese into a simple risotto just before you eat it makes it taste heavenly – quite an explosion on the taste buds!

To make the risotto, put the stock in a saucepan and keep at a gentle simmer. Melt half the butter in a large, heavy saucepan and add the onion. Cook gently for 10 minutes until soft, golden and translucent but not browned. Add the rice and stir until well coated with butter and heated through. Add the wine, if using, and boil hard until it has reduced and almost disappeared.

Begin adding the stock, a ladleful at a time, stirring gently until each one has been almost absorbed into the rice. The risotto should be kept at a bare simmer throughout cooking, so don't let the rice dry out – add more stock as necessary. Continue until the rice is tender and creamy, but the grains still firm. (This should take 15–20 minutes, depending on the type of rice used.) Season well with salt and pepper and beat in the remaining butter. Cover and let rest for a couple of minutes so the risotto can relax.

Serve in warm bowls with a large spoonful of pesto in each or spoon liquid pesto over the entire surface before serving, as preferred.

making pesto genovese step-by-step

2 garlic cloves

50 g/½ cup pine nuts

50 g/1¼ cups fresh basil leaves

150 ml/⅔ cup extra virgin olive oil (or more)

50 g/4 tablespoons unsalted butter, softened

4 tablespoons freshly grated Parmesan

sea salt and freshly ground black pepper

MAKES 250 ML/1 CUP

Don't stint on the fresh basil here – to make good pesto, you must use the right amount of very fresh basil leaves – too little basil and it will taste insipid. Adding a little softened butter at the end gives the pesto a delicious creaminess. This recipe makes a thick sauce: if you would prefer a lake of it floating over the surface of your risotto, then simply add more olive oil. Homemade pesto can be frozen successfully – some suggest leaving out the cheese and beating it in when the pesto has thawed, but I have never had any problems including it in the beginning.

(1) Peel the garlic and put it in a mortar with a little salt and the pine nuts. Pound with a pestle until broken up.

(2) Add the basil leaves, a few at a time, pounding and mixing to a paste.

(3) Gradually beat in the olive oil, little by little, until the mixture is creamy and thick.

(4) Beat in the butter and season with pepper, then beat in the Parmesan.

Use immediately or spoon into a screwtop jar (with a layer of olive oil on top of the pesto to exclude the air) and store in the refrigerator for up to 2 weeks or freeze for up to 3 weeks.

parmesan and butter risotto

risotto alla parmigiana

When you have nothing except risotto rice, a chunk of Parmesan (ideally real Parmigiano Reggiano) and some butter to work with, yet feel the need for comfort and luxury, this is the risotto for you. It is pale, golden, smooth and creamy and relies totally on the quality of these three ingredients. That said, if you find you also have some fresh or frozen peas and some pieces of diced pancetta (cured pork belly meat) or cubed thick ham to hand, you can stir these in at the end with the butter and Parmesan to add a little extra pep.

about 1.5 litres/6 cups hot Vegetable Stock (page 149) or Chicken Stock (page 150)

150 g/1 stick plus 3 tablespoons unsalted butter

1 onion, finely chopped

500 g/2⅓ cups risotto rice, preferably carnaroli

150 ml/⅔ cup dry white wine

100 g/1 cup freshly grated Parmesan

sea salt and freshly ground black pepper

SERVES 4–6

Put the stock in a saucepan and keep at a gentle simmer. Melt half the butter in a large, heavy saucepan and add the onion. Cook gently for 10 minutes until soft, golden and translucent but not browned. Add the rice and stir until well coated with the butter and heated through. Pour in the wine and boil hard until it has reduced and almost disappeared. This will remove any raw alcohol taste.

Begin adding the stock, a large ladleful at a time, stirring gently until each ladle has almost been absorbed by the rice. The risotto should be kept at a bare simmer throughout cooking, so don't let the rice dry out – add more stock as necessary. Continue until the rice is tender and creamy, but the grains still firm. (This should take 15–20 minutes depending on the type of rice used.)

Taste and season well with salt and pepper, then stir in the remaining butter and all the Parmesan. Cover and let rest for a couple of minutes so the risotto can relax and the cheese melt, then serve immediately. You may like to add a little more stock just before you serve, but don't let the risotto wait around too long or the rice will turn mushy.

saffron risotto
risotto allo zafferano

This is not to be confused with *risotto alla milanese*, which accompanies the famous dish osso buco, enriched with delicious beef bone marrow. However, this recipe does the job very nicely, producing a rich, creamy risotto with the delicate taste of saffron. Saffron powder can also be used, but make sure it is real saffron and not just ground stamens of the safflower. Saffron will always be relatively expensive when bought outside its country of origin, and is a great thing to take home with you if you are visiting Italy or Spain, where it can be found at a good price.

Put the stock in a saucepan and keep at a gentle simmer. Melt half the butter in a large, heavy saucepan and add the onion. Cook gently for 10 minutes until soft, golden and translucent but not browned. Add the rice and stir until well coated with the butter and heated through. Pour in the wine and boil hard until it has reduced and almost disappeared. This will remove any raw alcohol taste.

Begin adding the stock, a large ladleful at a time, adding the saffron after the first ladle. Stir gently until each ladle has almost been absorbed by the rice. The risotto should be kept at a bare simmer throughout cooking, so don't let the rice dry out – add more stock as necessary. Continue until the rice is tender and creamy, but the grains still firm. (This should take about 15–20 minutes depending on the type of rice used.)

Season well with salt and pepper and stir in the remaining butter and all the Parmesan. Cover and let rest for a couple of minutes so the risotto can relax, then serve immediately. You may like to add a little more stock just before serving to loosen it, but don't let the risotto wait around too long or the rice will turn mushy.

about 1.5 litres/6 cups hot Vegetable Stock (page 149) or Chicken Stock (page 150)

125 g/1 stick unsalted butter

1 onion, finely chopped

500 g/2⅓ cups risotto rice

150 ml/⅔ cup dry white wine

16 saffron threads or ½ teaspoon ground saffron

75 g/¾ cup freshly grated Parmesan

sea salt and freshly ground black pepper

SERVES 4–6

red wine risotto

risotto al barolo

An amazing risotto to serve on its own as a first course or to accompany meat or game dishes. This risotto needs the sweetness of the vegetables to balance the acidity from the wine. Use a good wine that you would not be ashamed to drink, and you will achieve perfect results. If you opt for a cheap, undrinkable wine, the risotto will be inedible. Brighten it up with a scattering of emerald-green chopped flat-leaf parsley.

about 1.5 litres hot Vegetable Stock (page 149) or Chicken Stock (page 150)

125 g/1 stick unsalted butter

1 small red onion, finely chopped

1 small carrot, finely chopped

1 small celery stalk/rib, finely chopped

50 g/2 oz. pancetta, finely chopped (optional)

500 g/2⅓ cups risotto rice

300 ml/1⅓ cups full-bodied red wine such as Barolo

125 g/1¼ cups freshly grated Parmesan

sea salt and freshly ground black pepper

chopped fresh flat-leaf parsley, to serve

SERVES 4–6

Put the stock in a saucepan and keep at a gentle simmer. Melt half the butter in a large, heavy saucepan and add the onion, carrot and celery. Cook gently for 10 minutes until soft, golden and translucent but not browned. Add the pancetta (if using) and cook for another 2 minutes. Add the rice and stir until well coated with the butter and heated through. Pour in the wine and boil hard until it has been reduced by half. This will remove the taste of raw alcohol.

Begin adding the stock, a large ladleful at a time, stirring gently until each ladle has almost been absorbed by the rice. The risotto should be kept at a bare simmer throughout cooking, so don't let the rice dry out – add more stock as necessary. Continue until the rice is tender and creamy, but the grains still firm. (This should take 15–20 minutes depending on the type of rice used.)

Taste and season well with salt and pepper and beat in the remaining butter and all the Parmesan. Cover and let rest for a couple of minutes so the risotto can relax, then serve immediately. You may like to add a little more hot stock to the risotto just before you serve to loosen it, but don't let it wait around too long or the rice will turn mushy. Serve sprinkled with parsley.

green herb risotto with white wine and lemon

risotto alle erbe verdi e limone

A wonderfully light and fragrant risotto, perfect for the summer to serve with cold chicken or fish. Try to use the more fragrant soft green herbs here – the more the merrier.

Put the stock in a saucepan and keep at a gentle simmer. Melt half the butter in a large, heavy saucepan and add the spring onions/scallions. Cook gently for 3–5 minutes until soft. Pour in the wine, add half the lemon zest and boil hard until the wine has reduced and almost disappeared. This will remove the taste of raw alcohol. Add the rice and stir until well coated with butter and onions and heated through.

Begin to add the hot stock, a large ladleful at a time, stirring until each ladle has been absorbed by the rice. Continue until the rice is tender and creamy, but the grains still firm. (This should take 15–20 minutes depending on the type of rice used.)

Taste and season well with salt and lots of freshly ground black pepper. Stir in the remaining butter and lemon zest, the lemon juice, herbs and Parmesan. Cover and let rest for a couple of minutes, then serve immediately.

about 1.5 litres/6 cups hot Vegetable Stock (page 149) or Chicken Stock (page 150)

125 g/1 stick unsalted butter

8 spring onions/scallions, green and white parts, finely chopped

150 ml/⅔ dry white wine

finely grated zest and juice of 1 large unwaxed lemon

500 g/2⅓ cups risotto rice

4 tablespoons chopped fresh herbs such as flat-leaf parsley, basil, marjoram and thyme

75 g/¾ cup freshly grated Parmesan

sea salt and freshly ground black pepper

SERVES 4–6

VEGETABLES

simple tomato and basil risotto

risotto al pomodoro e basilico

It's hard to beat a simple risotto made with fresh seasonal ingredients. Here summer-ripe tomatoes and sweet, liquoricy basil are stirred into buttery semi-cooked rice; the rice should be a little softened around the edges but still firm to the bite.

Cut the tomatoes in half and squeeze out and discard as many seeds as possible. Finely dice the flesh and set aside.

Put the stock and vermouth in a medium saucepan set over low heat. Put half of the butter and the oil in a heavy-based saucepan and set over medium heat. Add the garlic and leek and cook for 4–5 minutes, until softened. Add the rice and cook for 1 minute, until shiny and glossy.

Add about 60 ml/4 tablespoons of the hot stock mixture to the rice and stir constantly, until almost all of the liquid has been absorbed. Add another 60 ml/ 4 tablespoons to the pan, stirring until almost all the liquid has been absorbed. Continue adding the stock mixture a little at a time and stirring, until all the stock has been used and the rice is just tender.

Stir in the tomatoes, basil, Parmesan and remaining butter until well combined. Drizzle with olive oil and serve immediately.

3 fresh plum tomatoes

1 litre/4 cups hot Vegetable Stock (page 149)

4 tablespoons dry vermouth

30 g/2 tablespoons unsalted butter

2 tablespoons olive oil

2 garlic cloves, chopped

1 large trimmed leek, sliced

325 g/generous 1½ cups risotto rice

a large handful of fresh basil leaves, roughly torn

50 g/½ cup freshly grated Parmesan

extra virgin olive oil, to drizzle

SERVES 4

spinach and rocket risotto with roast tomatoes

risotto con spinaci, rucola e pomodori

This simple risotto makes the most of young spinach and peppery rocket/arugula, but watercress makes a good alternative if you can't find it. Even if you hate anchovies, don't leave them out. They will dissolve into nothing, but add a salty, savoury flavour to the heart of the risotto. If you are a vegetarian, you could add a dash of soy sauce to the stock instead.

about 1.5 litres/6 cups hot Vegetable Stock (page 149)

125 g/1 stick unsalted butter

1 onion, finely chopped

1 salted anchovy, boned, split and rinsed, or 2 anchovy fillets in oil

400 g/2 cups risotto rice

150 ml/⅔ cup dry white wine

400 g/1 lb. baby plum tomatoes

4 tablespoons olive oil

200 g/8 oz. young fresh spinach leaves, washed and drained

50 g/2 oz. fresh rocket/arugula leaves

sea salt and freshly ground black pepper

freshly grated Parmesan, to serve

SERVES 4

Put the stock in a saucepan and keep at a gentle simmer. Melt half the butter in a large, heavy saucepan and add the onion and anchovy. Cook gently for 10 minutes until soft, golden and translucent but not browned. Add the rice and stir until well coated with the butter and heated through. Pour in the wine and boil hard to reduce until it has almost disappeared. This will remove the taste of raw alcohol. Remove from the heat.

Put the tomatoes in a roasting tin/pan and sprinkle with olive oil. Mix well to coat, then season with salt and pepper. Roast in a preheated oven at 200°C (400°F) Gas 6 for about 20 minutes or until slightly collapsed with the skins beginning to brown. Remove from the oven and set aside.

Return the risotto to the heat, warm through and begin adding the stock, a large ladleful at a time, stirring gently until each ladle has been almost absorbed into the rice. The risotto should be kept at a bare simmer throughout cooking, so don't let the rice dry out – add more stock as necessary. Continue until the rice is tender and creamy, but the grains still firm. (This should take between 15–20 minutes depending on the type of rice used.) Just before the risotto is cooked, stir in the spinach and rocket/arugula. Taste and season well with salt and pepper and beat in the remaining butter and the Parmesan. You may like to add a little more hot stock to the risotto at this stage to loosen it. Cover and let rest for a couple of minutes so the risotto can relax, the cheese melt and the spinach and rocket/arugula wilt. Fold in the tomatoes and juices and serve immediately.

triple tomato risotto with fresh basil

risotto ai tre pomodori

Tomato and rice soup at its best! The risotto is full of the intense flavour of tomatoes, added in three ways: passata to the stock; sun-dried tomatoes adding their caramel flavour deep in the risotto; then tiny ripe plum tomatoes, roasted to perfect sweetness. Delicious hot – but the leftovers are marvellous eaten straight out of the pan.

Put the plum tomatoes in a roasting pan and pour over the olive oil. Toast to coat and season with salt and pepper. Roast in a preheated oven at 200°C (400°F) Gas 6 for about 20 minutes, until they are slightly collapsed and the skins beginning to brown. Remove from the oven and set aside.

Meanwhile, pour the stock and passata into a saucepan, stir well, then heat to a gentle simmer. Melt half the butter in a large, heavy saucepan and add the onion and chopped sun-dried tomatoes. Cook gently for 10 minutes until soft, golden and translucent but not browned. Add the rice and stir until well coated with the butter and heated through. Pour in the wine and boil hard until it has reduced and almost disappeared.

Begin adding the stock, a large ladleful at a time, stirring gently until each ladleful has almost been absorbed by the rice. The risotto should be kept at a bare simmer throughout cooking, so don't let the rice dry out – add more stock as necessary. Continue until the rice is tender and creamy, but the grains still firm (15–20 minutes depending on the type of rice used).

Season to taste, beat in the remaining butter, the Parmesan and chopped basil. You may like to add a little more hot stock at this stage to loosen the risotto – it should be quite wet. Cover and let rest for a couple of minutes so the risotto can relax and the cheese melt. Carefully ladle into warm bowls and cover the surface with the roasted tomatoes and any juices. Add the basil leaves and serve immediately with extra freshly grated Parmesan.

450 g/1lb. whole baby plum tomatoes

4 tablespoons olive oil

about 1 litre/4 cups hot Vegetable Stock (page 149)

500 ml/2 cups passata (Italian sieved/strained tomatoes)

125 g/1 stick unsalted butter

1 onion, finely chopped

8 pieces sun-dried tomatoes (not the ones in oil), chopped

400 g/2 cups risotto rice, preferably vialone nano

150 ml/⅔ cup light red wine

50 g/½ cup freshly grated Parmesan

4 tablespoons chopped fresh basil

sea salt and freshly ground black pepper

extra basil leaves and freshly grated Parmesan, to serve

SERVES 4

beetroot risotto with grilled radicchio

risotto con barbabietole e radicchio arrostito

A spectacular risotto, full of earthy sweetness which comes from finely chopped beetroot/beet. Using raspberry vinegar instead of wine is a good tip, as long as you don't use too much. The raspberry complements the beetroot and the vinegar keeps the red onion pink. I serve this topped with grilled/broiled radicchio and melting Fontina cheese for contrast of sweet and bitter.

about 1.5 litres/6 cups hot Vegetable Stock (page 149)

500 g/1 lb. raw beetroot/beet, peeled and chopped into small cubes

125 g/1stick unsalted butter

1 red onion, finely chopped

3 tablespoons raspberry vinegar or red wine vinegar

500 g/2⅓ cups risotto rice

200 g/2 cups Fontina cheese, grated

3 tablespoons chopped fresh flat-leaf parsley

sea salt and freshly ground black pepper

grilled/broiled radicchio (optional)

3 small radicchio, quartered lengthwise

100 ml/½ cup olive oil

SERVES 6

Pour the stock into a saucepan and keep at a gentle simmer on top of the stove. Add the beetroot/beet and simmer for 20–30 minutes until almost tender. Lift out the beetroot with a slotted spoon and set aside.

Melt half the butter in a large, heavy saucepan and add the onion and vinegar. Cook gently for 10 minutes until soft, golden and translucent, but not browned. Add the cooked beetroot, then the rice and stir until well coated with butter and heated through. Begin adding the stock, a large ladleful at a time, stirring gently until each ladle has almost been absorbed by the rice. The risotto should be kept at a bare simmer throughout cooking, so don't let the rice dry out – add more stock as necessary. Continue until the rice is tender and creamy, but the grains still firm. (This should take 15–20 minutes depending on the type of rice used.) Taste and season well with salt and pepper and beat in the remaining butter, Fontina and parsley. Cover and let rest for a couple of minutes so the risotto can relax and the cheese melt, then serve immediately.

If serving with the radicchio, heat a grill/broiler. Put the radicchio pieces in a grill pan and brush with the oil. Grill/broil for 10–15 minutes until soft and beginning to colour, turning a couple of times. Remove from the grill/broiler and set aside. Stir half the Fontina into the risotto before resting. Ladle the risotto into 4 heatproof bowls and top each one with 2 radicchio quarters. Sprinkle with the remaining Fontina, set on a baking sheet and grill/broil for 5 minutes until the cheese is melted and bubbling. Serve immediately.

butternut squash, sage and chilli risotto

risotto alla zucca, salvia e peperoncino

I live in Scotland and was tempted to make a traditional pumpkin risotto using what we call 'turnip' (swede) instead. I was impressed with the result. It was less sweet and cloying than it would be using pumpkin or squash, but had a very distinct flavour. I have served this on Burns' Night on 25th January with haggis, and it is delicious – to my taste anyway – but stick to the traditional recipe and it will be just as good. This tastes wonderful on its own or served with grilled meats.

Pour the stock into a saucepan and keep at a gentle simmer. Melt half the butter in a large, heavy saucepan and add the onion. Cook gently for 10 minutes until soft, golden and translucent but not browned. Stir in the chopped chillies and cook for 1 minute. Add the butternut or pumpkin, and cook, stirring constantly over the heat for 5 minutes, until it begins to soften slightly. Stir in the rice to coat with the butter and vegetables. Cook for a few minutes to toast the grains.

Begin adding the stock, a large ladleful at a time, stirring gently until each ladle has almost been absorbed by the rice. The risotto should be kept at a bare simmer throughout cooking, so don't let the rice dry out – add more stock as necessary. Continue until the rice is tender and creamy, but the grains still firm and the squash beginning to disintegrate. (This should take 15–20 minutes depending on the type of rice used.)

Taste and season well with salt and pepper and stir in the sage, remaining butter and all the Parmesan. Cover, let rest for a couple of minutes, then serve immediately.

about 1.5 litres/6 cups hot Vegetable Stock (page 149) or Chicken Stock (page 150)

125 g/1 stick unsalted butter

1 large onion, finely chopped

1–2 fresh or dried red chillies, deseeded and finely chopped

500 g/1 lb. fresh butternut squash or pumpkin (or swede), peeled and finely diced

500 g/2⅓ cups risotto rice

3 tablespoons chopped fresh sage

75 g/¾ cups freshly grated Parmesan

sea salt and freshly ground black pepper

SERVES 6

pumpkin and pea risotto with toasted pumpkin seeds

risotto alla zucca e piselli

A pretty orange colour speckled with vivid green peas, this risotto is a delight to eat – the peas pop in your mouth and the seeds give crunch. Fresh peas in season are fantastic, but I am a fan of frozen peas and am never ashamed to use them.

125 g/1 stick unsalted butter

3 tablespoons pumpkin seeds

¼–½ teaspoon chilli/chili powder

about 1 litre/4 cups hot Vegetable Stock (page 149) or Chicken Stock (page 150)

1 large onion, finely chopped

500 g/1 lb. fresh pumpkin or butternut squash, peeled and finely diced

300 g/1½ cups risotto rice

3 tablespoons chopped fresh mint

200 g/1½ cups frozen peas, cooked and drained

75 g/¾ cup freshly grated Parmesan

sea salt and freshly ground black pepper

SERVES 6

Put half the butter in a saucepan, melt until foaming, then add the pumpkin seeds. Stir over medium heat until the seeds begin to brown, then stir in the chilli/chili powder, salt and pepper. Remove from the heat and keep them warm.

Put the stock in a saucepan and keep at a gentle simmer. Melt the remaining butter in a large, heavy saucepan and add the onion. Cook gently for 10 minutes until soft, golden and translucent but not browned. Add the squash or pumpkin, and cook, stirring constantly over the heat for 15 minutes until it begins to soften and disintegrate. Mash the pumpkin in the pan with a potato masher. Stir in the rice to coat with the butter and mashed pumpkin. Cook for a couple of minutes to toast the grains.

Begin adding the stock, a large ladleful at a time, stirring gently until each ladle has almost been absorbed by the rice. The risotto should be kept at a bare simmer throughout cooking, so don't let the rice dry out – add more stock as necessary. Continue until the rice is tender and creamy, but the grains still firm. (This should take 15–20 minutes depending on the type of rice used.)

Taste and season well with salt and pepper and stir in the mint, peas and all the Parmesan. Cover and let rest for a couple of minutes so the risotto can relax, then serve immediately, sprinkled with the pumpkin seeds.

courgette flower risotto
risotto con fiori di zucchine

This is a pretty, delicate risotto made even more special with sliced courgette flowers/squash blossom. There are two types of blossom – male and female. The female flowers will produce a courgette/zucchini if fertilized, while the male flowers can be stuffed. They are just a flower on a stalk and the central spike must be removed before cooking. Courgette flowers/squash blossoms are sold in Italian greengrocers and farmers' markets.

Put the stock in a saucepan and keep at a gentle simmer. Melt half the butter in a large, heavy saucepan and add the onion and celery. Cook gently for 10 minutes until soft, golden and translucent but not browned. Add the rice and stir until well coated with the butter and heated through.

Begin adding the stock, a large ladleful at a time, stirring gently until each ladle has almost been absorbed by the rice. The risotto should be kept at a bare simmer throughout cooking, so don't let the rice dry out – add more stock as necessary. Halfway through cooking, stir in the grated courgettes/zucchini. Continue cooking and adding stock until the rice is tender and creamy, but the grains still firm. (This should take about 15–20 minutes, depending on the type of rice used.)

Taste and season well with salt and pepper, beat in the remaining butter and all the Parmesan, then stir in the courgette flowers/squash blossom. Cover and let rest for a couple of minutes so the risotto can relax, then serve immediately.

about 1.5 litres/6 cups hot Vegetable Stock (page 149) or Chicken Stock (page 150)

125 g/1 stick unsalted butter

1 onion, finely chopped

1 celery stick/rib, finely chopped

400 g/2 cups risotto rice

4 courgettes/zucchini, grated

50 g/½ cup freshly grated Parmesan

4–6 courgette flowers/squash blossom, trimmed and finely sliced

sea salt and freshly ground black pepper

SERVES 4

wild mushroom risotto

risotto ai funghi di bosco

We make this risotto in our cooking classes in Tuscany in October, when fresh porcini mushrooms are around – and it's a great favourite. Any kind of fresh wild mushroom will make this taste wonderful – black trompettes de mort, deep golden girolles or musky chanterelles. However, it can be made very successfully using a mixture of cultivated mushrooms and reconstituted dried Italian porcini or French cèpes. In Italy, a wild herb called nepitella is often used when cooking wild mushrooms. It is a type of wild catnip and complements the mushrooms very well.

about 1.5 litres/6 cups hot Vegetable Stock (page 149) or Chicken Stock (page 150)

125 g/1 stick unsalted butter

1 large onion, finely chopped

2 garlic cloves, finely chopped

250 g/3 cups mixed wild mushrooms, well cleaned and coarsely chopped (or a mixture of wild and fresh, or 200 g/1½ cups cultivated mushrooms, plus 25 g/1 oz. dried porcini soaked in warm water for 20 minutes, drained and chopped)

1 tablespoon each of chopped fresh thyme and marjoram (or nepitella)

150 ml/⅔ cup dry white wine or vermouth

500 g/2⅓ cups risotto rice

75 g/¾ cup freshly grated Parmesan, plus extra to serve

sea salt and freshly ground black pepper

SERVES 6

Put the stock in a saucepan and keep at a gentle simmer. Melt the butter in a large, heavy saucepan and add the onion and garlic. Cook gently for 10 minutes until soft, golden and translucent but not browned. Stir in the mushrooms and herbs, then cook over medium heat for 3 minutes to heat through. Pour in the wine and boil hard until it has reduced and almost disappeared. Stir in the rice and fry with the onion and mushrooms until dry and slightly opaque.

Begin adding the stock, a large ladleful at a time, stirring until each ladle has been absorbed by the rice. Continue until the rice is tender and creamy, but the grains still firm. (This should take 15–20 minutes depending on the type of rice used.)

Taste and season well with salt and pepper. Stir in the Parmesan, cover and let rest for a couple of minutes. Serve immediately with plenty of extra grated Parmesan.

wild mushroom and leek risotto

risotto ai fungi e porri senza lattosio

It's nice to think that a dish you associate with butter, cream and Parmesan can be just as enjoyable and indulgent when made with dairy-free alternatives. This recipe uses soy cream/ creamer to give it that velvety smoothness. It has the same consistency as normal cream, and the slight difference in taste is undetectable in the risotto when seasoned properly. If you can find them in a farmers' market, buy the amazing 'trompettes de la mort' mushrooms (trumpets of death).

Bring and keep the vegetable stock in a pan just under boiling point, ready to add into the risotto.

Heat the oil in a heavy-based pan, add the onion and leeks and cook gently over low heat until they are completely soft and translucent. You do not want to colour them. Add 5 of the chopped garlic cloves, turn up the heat and stir for 1 minute. Add the rice, stirring frequently until the grains are completely covered in oil and beginning to turn translucent.

Pour in the glass of wine (it should steam and bubble) and season with a pinch of salt. Gradually add the hot stock a ladleful at a time, adding another ladle each time the liquid has been absorbed by the rice. Continue until the rice is tender and creamy, but the grains still firm. (This should take 15–20 minutes depending on the type of rice used.) Stir through the soy cream/creamer and some pepper. Season to taste, then cover and turn off the heat.

In a separate pan, warm a little oil over medium–high heat. Add the mushrooms and fry for 1–2 minutes until the mushrooms have softened and coloured a little.

Add the mushrooms to the risotto. Make a quick parsley oil by combining the chopped parsley with the remaining chopped garlic clove and as much oil as you like. Drizzle over the risotto and serve immediately.

900 ml/3¾ cups hot Vegetable Stock (page 149)

3 tablespoons extra virgin olive oil, plus extra for the parsley oil

1 large onion, finely chopped

2 leeks, chopped

6 garlic cloves, finely chopped

350 g/1¾ cups risotto rice

125 ml/½ cup dry white wine

200 ml/¾ cup soy cream/creamer

300 g/10 oz. mixed wild mushrooms

3 tablespoons finely chopped parsley

sea salt and freshly ground black pepper

SERVES 6–8

oven-roasted mediterranean vegetable risotto

risotto con verdure del mediterraneo

The secret of this risotto is not to cut the vegetables too big – they should be jewel-like in the risotto. I stir half into the risotto, pile the rest on top and drizzle over good olive oil before serving.

Put the courgette/zucchini, aubergine/eggplant, bell pepper and carrot into a large roasting pan, add the oil and 100 ml/½ cup water and toss well to coat. Roast in a preheated oven at 200°C (400°F) Gas 6 for about 25 minutes, turning often until the vegetables are tender and caramelizing. Remove from the oven and tip into a colander set over a bowl. Reserve the cooking juices. Cool the vegetables.

Put the stock in a saucepan and keep at a gentle simmer. Melt half the butter in a large, heavy saucepan and add the onion, garlic and the lemon juice. Cook gently for 10 minutes until soft, golden and translucent but not browned. Add the coriander seeds and chilli/chili powder, then the rice and stir until well coated with the butter and heated through. Pour in the reserved roasting juices and wine and boil hard until they have reduced and almost disappeared.

Begin adding the stock, a large ladleful at a time, stirring gently until each ladle has almost been absorbed by the rice. The risotto should be kept at a bare simmer throughout cooking, so don't let the rice dry out – add more stock as necessary. Continue until the rice is tender and creamy, but the grains still firm. (This should take 15–20 minutes depending on the type of rice used.)

Taste and season with salt and pepper and beat in the rest of the butter. Reserve a few spoonfuls of the vegetables, then fold in the remainder and the sliced basil, cover and let rest for a few minutes so the risotto can relax and the vegetables heat through. Serve immediately. Top with the basil leaves, reserved vegetables, Parmesan and a drizzle of olive oil.

1 courgette/zucchini, trimmed and cut into 2 cm/1-inch chunks

1 aubergine/eggplant, trimmed and cut into 2 cm/1-inch chunks

1 red pepper/bell pepper, halved, seeded and cut into squares

1 carrot, cut into matchsticks

100 ml/½ cup olive oil

about 1.5 litres/6 cups hot Vegetable Stock (page 149)

100 g/7 tablespoons unsalted butter

1 red onion, finely chopped

2 garlic cloves, finely chopped

1 tablespoon freshly squeezed lemon juice

1 teaspoon crushed coriander seeds

a pinch of chilli/chili powder

500 g/2⅓ cups risotto rice

150 ml/⅔ cup dry white wine

3 tablespoons finely sliced fresh basil

sea salt and freshly ground black pepper

basil leaves, freshly grated Parmesan and extra virgin olive oil, to serve

SERVES 6

caramelized carrot risotto with watercress pesto

risotto con carote arrostite e pesto al crescione

Carrots are an underrated vegetable. When in their prime, they are sweet and juicy and roast perfectly. The pesto, which looks spectacular with the orange risotto, has a nutty, peppery taste.

about 1.5 litres/6 cups hot Vegetable Stock (page 149) or Chicken Stock (page 150)

125 g/1 stick unsalted butter

1 onion, finely chopped

400 g/2 cups risotto rice

150 ml/⅔ cup dry white wine

75 g/¾ cup freshly grated Parmesan

sea salt and freshly ground black pepper

roasted carrots

500 g/1 lb. carrots, peeled, then cut into chunky rounds or batons

4 tablespoons olive oil

watercress pesto

2 handfuls of watercress leaves, without stalks

1 garlic clove, chopped

3 tablespoons freshly grated Parmesan

25 g/¼ cup shelled hazelnuts

90 ml/⅓ cup extra virgin olive oil, plus extra for covering

SERVES 4

First roast the carrots. Preheat the oven to 200°C (400°F) Gas 6. Toss the carrots in the olive oil, spread them out in a single layer in a roasting pan and sprinkle with salt and pepper. Roast in the preheated oven for about 20 minutes, turning occasionally until they begin to caramelize.

Meanwhile, to make the pesto, put the watercress, garlic, Parmesan, hazelnuts, olive oil, salt and pepper in a food processor and blend until smooth, scraping down any bits that cling to the side of the bowl. Alternatively, pound in a mortar with a pestle. Cover with a thin layer of oil and set aside.

To make the risotto, put the stock in a saucepan and keep at a gentle simmer. Melt half the butter in a large, heavy saucepan and add the onion. Cook gently for 10 minutes until soft, golden and translucent but not browned. Add the rice and stir until well coated with the butter and heated through. Pour in the wine and boil hard until it has reduced and almost disappeared. Begin adding the stock, a large ladleful at a time, stirring gently until each ladle has almost been absorbed by the rice. The risotto should be kept at a bare simmer throughout cooking, so don't let the rice dry out – add more stock as necessary. Continue until the rice is tender and creamy, but the grains still firm. (This should take 15–20 minutes depending on the type of rice used.) Stir in the carrots and pan juices. Add salt and pepper to taste and beat in the remaining butter and half the Parmesan.

Cover and let rest for a few minutes so the risotto can relax and the cheese melt, then serve immediately. Serve in warm bowls with a spoon of pesto on top and sprinkled with the remaining Parmesan.

fennel and black olive risotto

risotto ai finocchi con olive nere

A delicate fennel and lemon risotto with the taste of the Mediterranean stirred in just before serving. I like the rich earthiness of shiny, oven-dried black olives, but you can use large, juicy green olives.

To make the relish, heat 2 tablespoons of the olive oil in a saucepan and gently cook the onion, garlic and fennel for a few minutes until softening. Add the sun-dried tomatoes, olives and bay leaf and cook for 2–3 minutes more. Season to taste with salt and pepper, remove the bay leaf, then stir in the basil. Transfer to a food processor and blend to a coarse texture. Stir in the aniseed liqueur and remaining olive oil. Cover and set aside.

To make the risotto, put the stock in a saucepan and keep at a gentle simmer. Melt half the butter in a large, heavy saucepan and add the onion. Cook gently for 5 minutes until soft, golden and translucent, but not browned. Stir in the fennel and lemon zest and continue to cook for 10 minutes until softening. Add the rice and stir until well coated with the butter and heated through. Pour in the wine and boil hard until it has reduced and almost disappeared. This will remove the taste of raw alcohol.

Begin adding the stock, a large ladleful at a time, stirring gently until each ladle has almost been absorbed by the rice. The risotto should be kept at a bare simmer throughout cooking, so don't let the rice dry out – add more stock as necessary. Continue until the rice is tender and creamy, but the grains still firm and the fennel absolutely tender. (This should take about 15–20 minutes depending on the type of rice used.)

Taste and season well with salt and pepper and beat in the remaining butter. Cover and let rest for a couple of minutes so the risotto can relax, then serve immediately. Just before serving, you may like to add a little more hot stock to loosen the risotto, but don't let it wait around too long or the rice will turn mushy. Top with the fennel and black olive relish before serving with extra grated Parmesan.

about 1 litre/4 cups hot Vegetable Stock (page 149) or Chicken Stock (page 150)

125 g/1 stick unsalted butter

1 onion, finely chopped

3 fennel bulbs, trimmed and finely chopped (green tops included)

finely grated zest of 1 unwaxed lemon

300 g/1½ cups risotto rice

150 ml/⅔ cup dry white wine

freshly grated Parmesan, to serve

fennel and black olive relish

6 tablespoons extra virgin olive oil

1 onion, finely chopped

1 garlic clove, crushed

1 fennel bulb, trimmed and chopped

5 sun-dried tomatoes in oil, drained and coarsely chopped

200 g/1¼ cups oven-dried (Greek-style) black olives, pitted

1 fresh bay leaf

12 basil leaves, torn

2 tablespoons aniseed liqueur, such as Sambuca

sea salt and freshly ground black pepper

SERVES 6

spring risotto with herbs

risotto primavera alle erbe

The charm of this risotto is found in the delicate flavours and colours of spring. The vegetables are small and sweet, the herbs fresh and fragrant. Don't be tempted to skimp on the herbs here; as well as imparting intense flavour to the risotto, they add a beautiful colour. Sometimes I blend them with the remaining butter (melted) to give a bright green liquid to beat in at the end.

about 1.5 litres/6 cups hot Vegetable Stock (page 149) or Chicken Stock (page 150)

125 g/1 stick unsalted butter

6 spring onions/scallions, finely chopped

2 garlic cloves, crushed

150 g/1¼ cups cubed carrots, or a bunch of tiny new carrots, trimmed and scraped but kept whole

400 g/2 cups risotto rice, preferably carnaroli

100 g/4 oz. asparagus spears, trimmed and cut into 2-cm/1-inch lengths

100 g/4 oz. fine green beans, cut into 2-cm/1-inch lengths

100 g/4 oz. fresh or frozen peas or broad/fava beans, thawed if frozen

6 tablespoons chopped mixed fresh herbs, such as chives, dill, flat-leaf parsley, mint, chervil and tarragon

50 g/½ cup freshly grated Parmesan, plus extra to serve

sea salt and freshly ground black pepper

SERVES 4

Put the stock in a saucepan and keep at a gentle simmer. Melt half the butter in a large, heavy saucepan and add the spring onions/scallions, garlic and carrots. Cook gently for 5 minutes until the onions are soft and translucent but not browned. Stir in the rice until well coated with the butter and heated through.

Begin adding the stock, a large ladleful at a time, stirring gently until each ladle has almost been absorbed by the rice. The risotto should be kept at a bare simmer throughout cooking, so don't let the rice dry out – add more stock as necessary. After 10 minutes, add the asparagus, beans and peas and continue until the vegetables are tender and the rice is tender and creamy, but the grains still firm. (This should take 15–20 minutes depending on the type of rice used.)

Taste and season well with salt and pepper and stir in the remaining butter, the herbs and the Parmesan. Cover and let rest for a couple of minutes so the risotto can relax, then serve immediately with plenty of extra freshly grated Parmesan.

barley risotto with spring greens and radicchio

orzotto con vedure di primavera e radicchio

Using pearl barley instead of rice adds a nutty note to this risotto-style dish. You will often see spring greens and radicchio displayed side by side at farmers' markets – both look appealing, especially the boldly coloured radicchio, the 'painted lady' of the lettuce world. When used raw in salads it can be a little bitter, but when cooked in this risotto its flavour is softened.

Put the barley in a large, heatproof bowl and add sufficient boiling water to cover. Let sit for 10 minutes, just to soften the barley a little, then drain well and set aside.

Put the oil in a frying pan/skillet set over medium heat. Add the spring greens and radicchio and cook for 10 minutes, stirring often, until the leaves soften. Add the lemon zest and juice, stir well and set aside. Put the stock in a large saucepan set over low heat and gently warm through while you start the risotto.

Put half of the butter in a saucepan set over medium heat. Add the leek and garlic and cook for 4–5 minutes until the leeks are soft and silky. Add the barley and herbs and stir for 1 minute. Add a ladleful of the warmed stock and cook, stirring constantly, until almost all the stock has been absorbed. Repeat the process until all the stock has been incorporated and the barley is almost cooked through – the risotto will be quite wet. Add the spring greens, radicchio, remaining butter and Parmesan to the pan and stir well to combine. Sprinkle with parsley, if you like and serve with extra Parmesan on the side for sprinkling.

220 g/1¼ cups pearl barley

2 tablespoons light olive oil

500 g/1 lb. spring greens, roughly chopped

4 large radicchio leaves, torn

finely grated zest and freshly squeezed juice of 1 unwaxed lemon

1.25 litres/5 cups hot Vegetable Stock (page 149)

25 g/2 tablespoons butter

1 leek, thinly sliced

2 garlic cloves, chopped

2 teaspoons fresh thyme leaves

1 tablespoon fresh rosemary needles

50 g/½ cup freshly grated Parmesan, plus extra to serve

a handful of fresh flat-leaf parsley, chopped, to serve (optional)

SERVES 4

barley risotto with red wine and mushrooms

orzotto al vino rosso e funghi

Barley risotto, also known as 'barlotto', is one of my friend Nick Nairn's specialities. He loves to make this in autumn after mushroom-hunting near his cooking school on the Lake of Menteith in Scotland. I have always loved the chewy nuttiness of this recipe, which is made without the slow addition of stock. To make serving this dish easier, Nick suggests making it in advance and reheating it – something it does well, because unlike rice, barley doesn't go soggy with keeping.

3 tablespoons olive oil

175 g/scant 1 cup pearl barley, washed and drained

1 small onion, finely chopped

1 garlic clove, finely chopped

500 ml/2 cups hot Chicken Stock (page 150), Vegetable Stock (page 149) or water

1 tablespoon light soy sauce

150 ml/generous ½ cup red wine

300 g/10½ oz. fresh chanterelles (or other wild and cultivated mushrooms, such as porcini or portobellos)

75 g/¾ stick unsalted butter

2 tablespoons freshly chopped parsley

1 tablespoon freshly chopped tarragon

sea salt and freshly ground black pepper

SERVES 4

Heat the oil in a large saucepan, then add the barley and stir until it starts to turn golden (not brown) – this will take about 5 minutes. Add the onion and garlic and continue frying for 5–10 minutes, until the barley starts to brown. Don't let it burn, but you want a good, toasted flavour.

Add the stock, soy sauce, red wine, salt and pepper. Bring to the boil, turn down the heat, part-cover with a lid, then simmer gently until nearly all the liquid has been absorbed – this should take at least 30 minutes. The beauty of this one is that you don't need to stir it constantly.

Meanwhile, brush or scrape the mushrooms clean (slicing any bigger ones to size) and heat a frying pan until hot. Add two-thirds of the butter and all the mushrooms. Stir-fry over medium heat for 4–5 minutes, until lightly browned. Season with salt and pepper. Add the stir-fried mushrooms to the barley and mix gently. Remove from the heat and cover with kitchen foil with a few holes pierced in it to let the barley swell and absorb all the liquid. Leave it in a warm place for 15 minutes. (At this stage, you could let it cool, reheating it for serving up to 24 hours later.)

To serve, put the barley risotto pan back on the heat and beat in the parsley, tarragon and the remaining butter. Stir well until hot, add salt and pepper to taste and pile onto heated plates. Serve immediately.

CHEESE & EGGS

mozzarella and sun-blushed tomato risotto with basil

risotto con mozzarella e pomodori semi-secchi

When you dip your fork into this risotto, you will come across pockets of melting mozzarella. Mix in the tomato topping and you will make more strings. Try to use *mozzarella di bufala* – it has a fresh, lactic bite well-suited to this recipe.

about 1.5 litres/6 cups hot Vegetable Stock (page 149) or Chicken Stock (page 150)

125 g/1 stick unsalted butter

1 onion, finely chopped

400 g/2 cups risotto rice

150 ml/⅔ cup dry white wine

250 g/8 oz. mozzarella cut into 1-cm/½-inch cubes

4 tablespoons chopped fresh basil

300 g/10 oz. sun-blushed tomatoes

sea salt and freshly ground black pepper

extra basil leaves and freshly grated Parmesan, to serve

SERVES 4

Put the stock in a saucepan and keep at a gentle simmer. Melt half the butter in a large, heavy saucepan and add the onion. Cook gently for 10 minutes until soft, golden and translucent but not browned. Add the rice and stir until well coated with the butter and heated through. Pour in the wine and boil hard until it has reduced and almost disappeared. This will remove the taste of raw alcohol.

Begin adding the stock, a large ladleful at a time, stirring gently until each ladle has almost been absorbed by the rice. The risotto should be kept at a bare simmer throughout cooking, so don't let the rice dry out – add more stock as necessary. Continue until the rice is tender and creamy, but the grains still firm. (This should take 15–20 minutes depending on the type of rice used.)

Taste and season well with salt and pepper and beat in the remaining butter. You may like to add a little more hot stock at this stage to loosen the risotto. Fold in the cubed mozzarella and chopped basil. Cover and let rest for a couple of minutes so the risotto can relax and the cheese melt.

Carefully ladle into warm bowls and put a pile of tomatoes in the centre of each one. Top with basil leaves and serve immediately with freshly grated Parmesan.

gorgonzola and ricotta risotto with crisp sage leaves

risotto al gorgonzola, ricotta e salvia

Gorgonzola is a strong cheese with blue-green marbling. The mould is injected into the cheese and left in a temperature-controlled environment. Factory-made cheese is firmer, with a regular crazing of blue-green. Artisan Gorgonzola, left in caves to develop the mould naturally, produces a creamy, less densely marbled cheese. In Italy, you buy Gorgonzola either *dolce* or *piccante* – mild or strong.

To make the crisp sage leaves, heat the oil to 180°C (350°F) in a deep-fryer or wok. If using a fryer, put the leaves in the basket and lower into the oil. It will hiss alarmingly, but don't worry. Immediately the hissing has stopped, lift the basket out and shake off the excess oil. (If using a wok, use tongs or a slotted spoon.) Put the leaves on paper towels to drain. Season with a sprinkling of salt and set aside to cool.

Put the stock in a saucepan and keep at a gentle simmer. Melt half the butter in a large, heavy saucepan and add the onion. Cook gently for 10 minutes until soft, golden and translucent but not browned. Add the rice and stir until well coated with the butter and heated through. Pour in the vermouth and boil hard until reduced and almost disappeared. Stir in the chopped fresh sage.

Begin adding the stock, a large ladleful at a time, stirring gently until each ladle has almost been absorbed by the rice. The risotto should be kept at a bare simmer throughout cooking, so don't let the rice dry out – add more stock as necessary. About halfway through the cooking time, stir in the Gorgonzola until melted. Continue adding stock and cooking until the rice is tender and creamy, but the grains still firm. (This should take about 15–20 minutes depending on the type of rice used.) Taste and season well with salt and pepper and beat in the ricotta and remaining butter. Cover and let rest for a couple of minutes so the risotto can relax. Serve with the fried sage leaves on top.

about 1.5 litres/6 cups hot Vegetable Stock (page 149) or Chicken Stock (page 150)

125 g/1 stick unsalted butter

1 onion, finely chopped

400 g/2 cups risotto rice

75 ml/⅓ cup dry white vermouth

1 tablespoon chopped fresh sage leaves

75 g/¾ cup crumbled Gorgonzola

75 g/¾ cup fresh ricotta

sea salt and freshly ground black pepper

crisp sage leaves

about 30 sage leaves with stalks, rinsed and patted thoroughly dry

sea salt

light vegetable oil, for deep frying

electric deep-fryer or wok

SERVES 4

raclette or fontina risotto with bresaola

risotto alla raclette o fontina con bresaola

A risotto made with meltingly soft Fontina cheese or even raclette becomes almost a fondue. Bresaola is often served as a side dish with raclette and fondue, and makes a delicious topping to the risotto. Produced around Valtellina in Lombardy, bresaola is raw fillet of beef, salted then air-dried. It is always sliced very thinly and is a beautiful, deep garnet-red colour. Freshly cut bresaola is best, it is soft and sweet, whereas the layered kind in packets tends to be a bit dry.

about 1.5 litres/6 cups hot Vegetable Stock (page 149) or Chicken Stock (page 150)

125 g/1 stick unsalted butter

1 onion, finely chopped

500 g/2⅓ cups risotto rice

150 ml/⅔ cup fruity white wine

100 g/4 oz. Fontina or raclette cheese, rinds removed and remainder grated or chopped

6–8 thin slices bresaola, finely chopped, plus 8–12 thin slices extra, to serve

sea salt and freshly ground black pepper

SERVES 4–6

Put the stock in a saucepan and keep at a gentle simmer. Melt half the butter in a large, heavy saucepan and add the onion. Cook gently for 10 minutes until soft, golden and translucent but not browned. Add the rice and stir until well coated with the butter and heated through. Pour in the wine and boil hard until it has reduced and almost disappeared.

Begin adding the stock, a large ladleful at a time, stirring gently until each ladle has almost been absorbed by the rice. The risotto should be kept at a bare simmer throughout cooking, so don't let the rice dry out – add more stock as necessary. Halfway through cooking, stir in the cheese until melted. Continue adding stock and cooking until the rice is tender and creamy, but the grains still firm. (This should take about 15–20 minutes depending on the type of rice used.)

Taste and season well with salt and pepper and beat in the remaining butter and chopped bresaola. Cover and let rest for a couple of minutes so the risotto can relax.

Serve with the remaining bresaola crumpled or draped on top.

roasted garlic risotto with goats' cheese and rosemary

risotto con caprino, aglio dorato e rosmarino

I use two kinds of cheese in this indulgent risotto. The soft cheese melts creamily into the risotto, whereas the cheese with rind (*Bûcheron chèvre*) cut from a thick log, grills to perfection.

Preheat the oven to 180°C (350°F) Gas 4. Put the garlic and 2 tablespoons of oil in a mixing bowl, season and toss well. Put the garlic in the middle of the foil, fold up the long ends and fold together at the top to create a seal. Fold in the short ends to create a sealed packet. Set on a baking sheet and roast in the preheated oven for 20 minutes, then turn over, cut a small hole in the top and roast the packet upside down for a further 10 minutes.

Put the sliced goats' cheese on a grill pan lined with the parchment paper. Brush with olive oil and put a rosemary sprig on each one. Sprinkle with pepper and set aside. Preheat the grill/broiler.

Put the stock in a saucepan and keep at a gentle simmer. Heat the remaining olive oil in a heavy saucepan. Add the onion and cook gently for 5 minutes. Add 8 roasted garlic cloves and half the chopped rosemary. Cook for 5 minutes, then stir in the rice until well coated with oil and heated through.

Begin adding the stock, a ladleful at a time, stirring gently until each ladle has almost been absorbed by the rice. The risotto should be kept at a bare simmer throughout cooking – don't let the rice dry out and add more stock as necessary. Halfway through cooking time, grill/broil the sliced goats' cheese until browned on top. Continue until the rice is tender and creamy, but the grains still firm. (This should take about 15–20 minutes depending on the type of rice used.) Stir in the soft cheese and remaining rosemary.

Taste, season well and beat in the Parmesan. Cover and let rest for a couple of minutes so the risotto can relax, then serve immediately. Using a palette knife, set a slice of goats' cheese on each serving and top with a sprig of rosemary.

20 large garlic cloves, peeled (you will only use 8, but you can keep the rest in a jar of oil in the refrigerator)

75 ml/⅓ cup extra virgin olive oil, plus extra for basting

4–6 large thick slices goats' cheese with rind

4–6 small sprigs of rosemary, plus extra to serve

about 1.5 litres/6 cups hot Vegetable Stock (page 149) or Chicken Stock (page 150)

1 red onion, finely chopped

2 tablespoons chopped fresh rosemary

500 g/2⅓ cups risotto rice

200 g/8 oz. soft mild goats' cheese (the one with no rind)

50 g/½ cup freshly grated Parmesan

sea salt and freshly ground black pepper

30-cm/12-inch square of foil

a baking sheet

non-stick baking parchment

SERVES 4–6

truffled egg risotto

risotto all'uovo e tartufi

This is a way of enjoying the taste of truffles without the enormous expense. Fresh white truffles from Alba are heaven shaved over a white risotto, but there are lots of products flavoured with truffles. There's truffle butter, truffle oil (make sure it is the real thing and not just flavoured with a chemical) and truffle paste or sauce. All these can be mixed with egg yolks, then added to the risotto as long as you don't add too much – it can be very overpowering. Parsley brings the whole thing alive and the best parsley in Italy is said to come from Lombardy.

4 hard-boiled/cooked eggs

4 teaspoons truffle and porcini mushroom sauce or paste

about 1.5 litres/6 cups hot Vegetable Stock (page 149) or Chicken Stock (page 150)

125 g/1 stick unsalted butter

1 onion, finely chopped

400 g/2 cups risotto rice

2–3 tablespoons chopped fresh flat-leaf parsley

sea salt and freshly ground black pepper

flat-leaf parsley leaves, to serve

SERVES 4

Cut the eggs in half and take out the yolks. Finely chop the whites. Mash the yolks in a small bowl with the truffle and mushroom sauce or paste.

Put the stock in a saucepan and keep at a gentle simmer. Melt half the butter in a large, heavy saucepan and add the onion. Cook gently for 10 minutes until soft, golden and translucent but not browned. Add the rice and stir until well coated with the butter and heated through.

Begin adding the stock, a large ladleful at a time, stirring gently until each ladle has almost been absorbed by the rice. The risotto should be kept at a bare simmer throughout cooking, so don't let the rice dry out – add more stock as necessary. Continue until the rice is tender and creamy, but the grains still firm. (This should take about 15–20 minutes depending on the type of rice used.)

Taste and season well with salt and pepper and beat in the remaining butter, truffled egg yolks, chopped egg whites and the parsley. Cover and let rest for a couple of minutes so the risotto can relax, then serve immediately. You may like to add a little more hot stock to the risotto just before you serve to loosen it, but don't let it wait around too long or the rice will turn mushy. Serve topped with the flat-leaf parsley leaves.

creamy radicchio and mascarpone risotto

risotto cremoso al radicchio e mascarpone

Here is a dish from the Veneto, where vialone nano rice is grown, as well as several varieties of radicchio. Stirring in a good spoonful of mascarpone or cream at the end enriches the risotto and adds sweetness. The risotto has both a sweet and a bitter flavour. I like to add a few currants plumped up for 20 minutes in warm grappa for an added surprise.

Put the stock in a saucepan and keep at a gentle simmer. Melt half the butter in a large, heavy saucepan and add the carrots. Cook gently for 5 minutes until softening. Add the pancetta and garlic, and cook for 4 minutes until just beginning to colour. Stir in the radicchio and cook for 5 minutes until it begins to wilt.

Add the rice and stir until heated through. Add a ladleful of hot stock and simmer, stirring until absorbed. Continue adding the stock ladle by ladle, making sure the rice is never dry, until all the stock is absorbed. The rice should be tender and creamy but still have some bite to it. (This should take 15–20 minutes depending on the type of rice used.)

Taste and season well with salt and plenty of freshly ground black pepper. Add the grappa-soaked currants, if using, and stir in the remaining butter, the mascarpone or cream and the Parmesan. Cover and let rest for a couple of minutes so the risotto can relax, then serve immediately.

about 1.5 litres/6 cups hot Vegetable Stock (page 149) or Chicken Stock (page 150)

125 g/1 stick unsalted butter

2 carrots, finely diced

125 g/½ cup finely diced smoked pancetta

2 garlic cloves, finely chopped

500 g/1 lb. radicchio, finely shredded

500 g/2⅓ cups risotto rice

2 tablespoons currants soaked in 4 tablespoons warm grappa for 20 minutes (optional)

3 tablespoons mascarpone or double/heavy cream

75 g/¾ cup freshly grated Parmesan

sea salt and freshly ground black pepper

SERVES 6

asparagus risotto with a poached egg and parmesan

risotto agli asparagi con uovo in camicia e parmigiano

When the Italian asparagus season is in full flush, it is celebrated with great gusto. Asparagus of all types is for sale, the most prized being the fat white asparagus.

500 g/1 lb. fresh green or purple-tipped asparagus

about 1.5 litres/6 cups hot Vegetable Stock (page 149) or Chicken Stock (page 150)

1 teaspoon tarragon wine vinegar or white wine vinegar

6 fresh eggs, cracked into separate cups

125 g/1 stick unsalted butter

2 large shallots, finely chopped

500 g/2⅓ cups risotto rice, preferably carnaroli

50 g/½ cup freshly grated Parmesan

sea salt and freshly ground black pepper

to serve

1 tablespoon chopped fresh flat-leaf parsley and tarragon, mixed

Parmesan shavings

SERVES 6

Trim the base from each asparagus stem. Put the stock in a wide saucepan and heat to simmering point. Add the asparagus and boil for 6 minutes, or until just tender. Drain, reserving the stock and transferring it to a regular saucepan to simmer. Plunge the asparagus into a bowl of cold water to cool and set the colour, then cut into small pieces. If the ends of the asparagus stalks are very tough, cut them off, halve them and scrape out the insides and reserve. Add the tough parts to the stock. Reserve a few tips to serve.

To poach the eggs, fill a medium saucepan with cold water and bring to the boil. When the water is boiling, add the wine vinegar, then give it a good stir to create a whirlpool. Slip an egg into the vortex, then simmer very gently for 2–3 minutes. Using a slotted spoon, transfer the poached egg to a pan of warm water. Repeat the same procedure with the other eggs.

Melt half the butter in a large, heavy saucepan and add the shallots. Cook gently for 5–6 minutes until soft, golden and translucent but not browned. Add the rice and asparagus scrapings to the shallots and stir until well coated with the butter and heated through. Begin adding the stock, a large ladleful at a time (keeping back the asparagus trimmings), stirring gently until each ladle has almost been absorbed by the rice. The risotto should be kept at a bare simmer throughout cooking, so don't let the rice dry out – add more stock as necessary. Continue until the rice is tender and creamy, but the grains still firm. (This should take about 15–20 minutes depending on the type of rice used.)

Taste, season well and beat in the remaining butter and all the Parmesan. Fold in the drained asparagus. Cover, let rest for a few minutes then serve immediately topped with an egg and sprinkled with herbs and Parmesan.

artichoke and pecorino risotto

risotto ai carciofi e pecorino

Smoky char-grilled artichokes are wonderful combined with nutty pecorino. Pecorino is made from ewes' milk (*latte de pecora*) and when aged can be grated like Parmesan.

First prepare the fresh artichokes, if using (see below), then brush with olive oil and char-grill for 5 minutes on a stove-top grill pan, turning often. If using char-grilled ones from the deli, cut them in quarters and set aside. If using thawed frozen ones, slice them and fry in a little butter until golden.

Put the stock in a saucepan and keep at a gentle simmer. Melt half the butter in a large, heavy saucepan and add the onion. Cook gently for 10 minutes until soft, golden and translucent but not browned. Add the rice and stir until well coated with the butter and heated through. Pour in the wine and boil hard until it has reduced and almost disappeared.

Begin adding the stock, a large ladleful at a time, stirring gently until each ladle has almost been absorbed by the rice. Continue until the rice is tender and creamy, but the grains still firm. (This should take about 15–20 minutes depending on the type of rice used.) Taste, season well and beat in the remaining butter and all the pecorino. Fold in the artichokes. Cover and let rest for a couple of minutes so the risotto can relax, then serve immediately.

Note To prepare fresh young artichokes, you will need 1 fresh lemon, halved, and purple-green baby artichokes with stems and heads, about 10 cm/4 inches long. Fill a large bowl with water and squeeze in the juice of ½ lemon to acidulate it. Use the other lemon half to rub the cut portions of the artichoke as you work. Trim the artichokes by snapping off the dark outer leaves, starting at the base. Trim the stalk down to 5 cm/2 inches. Trim away the green outer layer at the base and peel the fibrous outside of the stalk with a vegetable peeler. Cut about 1 cm off the tip of each artichoke heart. Put each artichoke in the lemony water until needed, as this will stop them discolouring. Drain and use as required.

12 fresh artichokes, or 12 char-grilled deli artichokes, or 8 frozen artichoke bottoms, thawed

about 1.5 litres/6 cups hot Vegetable Stock (page 149) or Chicken Stock (page 150)

125 g/1 stick unsalted butter, plus extra for sautéing (optional)

1 onion, finely chopped

500 g/2⅓ cups risotto rice

150 ml/⅔ cup dry white wine

75 g/¾ cup freshly grated pecorino

sea salt and freshly ground black pepper

SERVES 4

POULTRY & GAME

chicken and mushroom risotto with tarragon

risotto al pollo, funghi e dragoncello

My favourite cultivated mushrooms are the large, flat, open, almost black portobellos. They have much more flavour than younger ones with closed caps, and are almost the next best thing to wild mushrooms. They absorb a lot of butter and I like to get them really quite brown to concentrate the flavour. Tarragon goes particularly well with this combination, but can be overpowering, so don't use too much.

250 g/8 oz. large portobello mushrooms

150 g/1 stick plus 3 tablespoons unsalted butter

1 garlic clove, finely chopped

about 1.5 litres/6 cups hot Chicken Stock (page 150)

1 onion, finely chopped

1 celery stalk/rib, finely chopped

600 g/1¼ lbs. boneless, skinless chicken thighs and breast, finely chopped

500 g/2⅓ cups risotto rice

300 ml/1¼ cups dry white wine

2 teaspoons chopped fresh tarragon

75 g/¾ cup freshly grated Parmesan

sea salt and freshly ground black pepper

chopped fresh flat-leaf parsley, to serve

SERVES 6

To prepare the mushrooms, cut them into long slices. Melt half the butter in a frying pan/skillet, add the mushrooms and garlic and sauté over medium heat until browning at the edges. Transfer to a plate and set aside.

Put the stock in a saucepan and keep at a gentle simmer. Melt half the remaining butter in a large, heavy saucepan and add the onion and celery. Cook gently for 10 minutes until soft and golden but not browned. Add the chicken and cook for another 5 minutes, but do not let it colour and harden. Stir in the rice until well coated with butter, heated through and beginning to smell 'toasted'. Pour in the wine, bring to the boil and boil hard to reduce by half – this will concentrate the flavour and remove the raw taste of alcohol.

Begin adding the stock, a large ladleful at a time, stirring gently until each ladle has been absorbed by the rice. The rice should always be at a gentle simmer. Continue in this way until the rice is tender and creamy, but the grains still firm. (This should take about 15–20 minutes depending on the type of rice used.)

Taste and season well with salt and pepper and stir in the remaining butter, the tarragon and Parmesan. Cover and let rest for a couple of minutes to let the risotto relax. Reheat the mushrooms, then serve the risotto with the mushrooms piled on top, sprinkled with chopped flat-leaf parsley.

chicken liver risotto with vin santo

risotto ai fegatini e vin santo

I first discovered the marriage of a little Vin Santo and chicken livers in Tuscany, when I was cooking a traditional topping of chicken livers for crostini. There wasn't an open bottle of wine handy, so I used a drop of Vin Santo. It was sublime. The sweet grapiness was perfect with chicken livers. Find the freshest, plumpest livers for this risotto.

Trim any stringy bits from the livers with a sharp knife. Cut away any discoloured bits and cut into large pieces. Set aside.

Put the stock in a saucepan and keep at a gentle simmer. Melt half the butter in a large, heavy saucepan and add the shallots, celery and carrot. Cook gently for 6–8 minutes until soft, golden and translucent but not browned. Stir in the livers, then raise the heat until they are cooked and firm on the outside, soft and pink inside. Stir in the Vin Santo and tomato paste and boil hard until the liquid has all but evaporated. Add the rice and stir until well coated with the butter and vegetables and heated through.

Begin adding the stock, a large ladleful at a time, stirring gently so as not to break up the chicken livers too much, until each ladle has almost been absorbed by the rice. The risotto should be kept at a bare simmer throughout cooking, so don't let the rice dry out – add more stock as necessary. Continue until the rice is tender and creamy, but the grains still firm. (This should take about 15–20 minutes depending on the type of rice used.)

Taste, season well and beat in the remaining butter, the capers and parsley. Cover and let rest for a couple of minutes so the risotto can relax, then serve immediately.

175 g/6 oz. plump fresh chicken livers

about 1.5 litres/6 cups hot Chicken Stock (page 150)

125 g/1 stick unsalted butter

2 shallots, finely chopped

1 celery stalk/rib, finely chopped

1 small carrot, finely chopped

3 tablespoons Italian Vin Santo or dry sherry

1 tablespoon sun-dried tomato paste or purée

400 g/2 cups risotto rice, preferably vialone nano

2 tablespoons salted capers, rinsed and chopped

3 tablespoons chopped fresh flat-leaf parsley

sea salt and freshly ground black pepper

SERVES 4

duck risotto with spinach
risotto all'anatra con spinaci

Make this risotto really soupy, with vialone nano rice, as served in the Veneto – the land of lagoons and wildfowl. Wild duck would make all the difference to this dish if you have access to it, giving it a rich, gamey taste. The anchovies are barely perceptible in the risotto, but they add a deep, savoury flavour, which will make even the most domestic of ducks taste like game birds. The balsamic vinegar is my secret ingredient, again to give depth to the finished dish.

about 1.5 litres/6 cups hot Game Stock made with duck bones (page 153) or Chicken Stock (page 150)

3 duck breasts with fat

125 g/1 stick unsalted butter or the skin from the duck breasts

1 onion, finely chopped

2 garlic cloves, finely chopped

100 g/½ cup chopped pancetta

1 tablespoon chopped fresh sage

1 tablespoon chopped fresh rosemary

finely grated zest and juice of 1 unwaxed lemon

2 anchovies in salt, cleaned, or 4 anchovy fillets, rinsed and chopped

150 ml/⅔ cup dry white wine (optional)

2 tablespoons balsamic vinegar

400 g/2 cups risotto rice, preferably *vialone nano*

200 g/7 oz. fresh young spinach, washed

sea salt and freshly ground black pepper

freshly grated Parmesan, to serve

SERVES 4

Put the stock in a saucepan and keep at a gentle simmer. Pull the fat off the duck breasts and chop it. Chop the duck meat into small pieces. Melt half the butter (or use the duck fat and skin and slowly fry it in the pan for 5–10 minutes until the fat melts, then remove the solids) in a large, heavy saucepan and add the onion and garlic. Cook for 10 minutes over medium heat until soft and beginning to caramelize.

Add the duck, pancetta, sage, rosemary, lemon zest and anchovies and cook for 2–3 minutes until changing colour, but not browning. Pour in the wine, if using, and balsamic vinegar and boil hard for 1 minute to boil off the alcohol. Add 2 ladlefuls of stock, cover and simmer very gently for about 20 minutes, until the duck is tender. Stir in the rice, then begin adding the stock, a large ladleful at a time, stirring gently until each ladle has almost been absorbed by the rice. The risotto should be kept at a bare simmer throughout cooking, so don't let the rice dry out – add more stock as necessary. Continue until the rice is tender and creamy, but the grains still firm. (This should take about 15–20 minutes depending on the type of rice used.)

Taste and season well with salt, pepper and lemon juice, beat in the remaining butter, then stir in the spinach. Cover and let rest for a couple of minutes so the risotto can relax and the spinach wilt, then serve immediately. Serve with freshly grated Parmesan.

pheasant and red wine risotto
risotto al fagiano e chianti

I was always excited when my father returned from a shoot with his game-bag full. Usually this meant pheasants, and this is one of the best ways to cook them. Roast pheasant is good too, but this is easier to eat and has all the wild, herby tastes of the hills.

Unless using boned breasts, remove the breasts and legs from the pheasants and set aside. Cut up the carcass and add to the stock with the bay leaves. Simmer for 30 minutes before you start, then strain the stock into a pan and keep at simmering point on the top of the stove.

Pull the skin off the breasts and legs and cut the flesh into small pieces, discarding any bones. Melt half the butter in a large, heavy saucepan and add the onion, carrot and celery (this is a *soffritto*). Cook gently for about 10 minutes, until soft and golden but not browned. Add the pancetta and pheasant and cook for another 5 minutes, but do not let it brown and harden. Stir in the rice until well coated with butter, heated through and beginning to smell toasted. Pour in the wine, bring to the boil and boil hard to reduce by half – this will concentrate the flavour and remove the raw taste of alcohol.

Begin adding the stock, a large ladleful at a time, stirring gently until each ladle has almost been absorbed by the rice. The risotto should be kept at a bare simmer throughout cooking, so don't let the rice dry out – add more stock as necessary. Continue until the rice is tender and creamy, but the grains still firm. (This should take 15–20 minutes depending on the type of rice used.)

Taste and season well with salt and pepper and stir in the remaining butter, the thyme and Parmesan. Cover and let rest for a couple of minutes so the risotto can relax, then serve immediately, sprinkled with chopped parsley.

3 prepared pheasants or
6 boned pheasant breasts

about 1.5 litres/6 cups hot Chicken Stock (page 150) or Game Stock (page 153)

2 bay leaves

125 g/1 stick unsalted butter

1 onion, finely chopped

1 carrot, finely chopped

1 celery stalk/rib, finely chopped

50 g/¼ cup finely chopped pancetta

500 g/2⅓ cups risotto rice

300 ml/1¼ cups red wine, such as Chianti

1 tablespoon chopped fresh thyme

75 g/¾ cup freshly grated Parmesan

sea salt and freshly ground black pepper

chopped fresh flat-leaf parsley, to serve

SERVES 6

hunter's-style rabbit risotto

risotto con coniglio alla cacciatora

This is a rich and earthy risotto, redolent of the hills of Tuscany or Umbria on an autumnal day. Farm-reared rabbit is such good value, very tender with a better texture than chicken, but wild rabbit has more flavour. I use all the ingredients from the famous dish *Coniglio alla Cacciatora* in this risotto.

about 1.5 litres/6 cups hot Chicken Stock (page 150) or Vegetable Stock (page 149)

125 g/1 stick unsalted butter

1 onion, finely chopped

1 carrot, finely chopped

1 celery stalk/rib, finely chopped

50 g/¼ cup finely chopped prosciutto

600 g/1¼ lbs. boneless rabbit, cut into small cubes

500 g/2⅓ cups risotto rice

1 tablespoon tomato purée/paste

150 ml/⅔ cup red wine, such as Chianti

1 tablespoon chopped fresh rosemary

150 g/6 oz. chestnut mushrooms, quartered

50 g/½ cup freshly grated Parmesan

50 g/¼ cup Greek-style (dry-cured) black olives, pitted and quartered

sea salt and freshly ground black pepper

sprigs of rosemary, to serve

SERVES 6

Put the stock in a saucepan and keep at a gentle simmer. Melt half the butter in a large, heavy saucepan and add the onion, carrot and celery. Cook gently for 10 minutes until soft and golden but not browned. Add the prosciutto and rabbit and cook for another 5 minutes, but do not let it colour and harden. Stir in the rice until well coated with butter, heated through and beginning to smell toasted. Mix the tomato purée with the wine and pour onto the rice. Bring to the boil and boil hard to reduce by half – this will concentrate the flavour and remove the raw taste of alcohol. Stir in the rosemary.

Begin adding the stock, a large ladleful at a time, stirring gently until each ladle has almost been absorbed by the rice. The risotto should be kept at a bare simmer throughout cooking, so don't let the rice dry out – add more stock as necessary. Halfway through cooking, stir in the mushrooms, then continue cooking, adding stock until the rice is tender and creamy, but the grains still firm. (This should take about 15–20 minutes depending on the type of rice used.)

Taste and season well with salt and pepper and stir in the remaining butter, the Parmesan and the olives. Cover and let rest for a couple of minutes so the risotto can relax, then serve immediately, topped with rosemary sprigs.

MEAT, SAUSAGE & BACON

risotto with meat sauce
risotto al ragù

Here, a classic meat ragù is transformed into a creamy risotto. It is important not to brown the meat and vegetables too much – this will turn the meat into hard little bullets. Cook the sauce very slowly, for as long as possible, 1–3 hours. The longer it simmers, the better it will taste.

ragù

100 g/7 tablespoons unsalted butter

300 g/10 oz. lean minced/ground beef, pork or veal

50 g/¼ cup minced or finely chopped prosciutto

1 small onion, finely chopped

1 small carrot, finely chopped

1 celery stalk/rib, finely chopped

3 tablespoons dry white wine

400 g/14 oz. tomato passata (sieved/strained Italian tomatoes)

1 tablespoon tomato purée/paste

about 2 litres/8 cups Beef or Veal Stock (page 153)

I bay leaf

sea salt and freshly ground black pepper

risotto

500 g/2⅓ cups risotto rice

75 g/¾ cup freshly grated Parmesan, plus extra to serve

sea salt and freshly ground black pepper

SERVES 6

To make the ragù, melt half the butter in a heavy casserole dish set over medium heat. Add the meat and prosciutto, onion, carrot and celery. Brown very lightly (you are not trying to sear the meat, just turn it from pink to pale grey-brown). Make sure you break it up as it cooks so that there are no large lumps. Add the wine, turn up the heat and boil until evaporated. Turn the heat down again. Add the passata and purée/paste, mix well, then add 500 ml/2 cups stock, the bay leaf, salt and pepper. Bring to the boil, stir well, then half-cover and turn the heat to a bare simmer. Simmer for about 2 hours or until the butter begins to separate on the surface: it should be rich and thick. Season to taste.

Set the remaining stock on the stove and keep at a gentle simmer. Stir the rice into the ragù, mixing well. Increase to a simmer. Begin adding the stock, a large ladleful at a time, stirring gently until each ladle has almost been absorbed by the rice. The risotto should be kept at a bare simmer throughout cooking, so don't let the rice dry out – add more stock as necessary. Continue until the rice is tender and creamy, but the grains still firm, about 15–20 minutes depending on the type of rice used.

Taste and season well, remove the bay leaf and beat in the remaining butter and Parmesan. Cover and let rest for a couple of minutes so the risotto can relax and the cheese melt, then serve immediately, sprinkled with the extra Parmesan.

artichoke risotto with lamb

risotto di carciofi con agnello

Artichokes are just made to go with lamb. Fresh smaller artichokes with a purple blush are best here, but you can use pared-down globe artichokes or the char-grilled ones sold in delis.

First prepare the fresh artichokes, if using. Brush with olive oil and char-grill for 5 minutes in a stove-top grill pan, turning often. Otherwise, quarter the bought char-grilled ones and set aside.

Preheat the oven to 220°C (425°F) Gas 7. Heat an ovenproof frying pan/skillet until very hot. Season the lamb well. Add the oil to the pan, then the lamb and a tablespoon of the butter and cook over high heat for 2–3 minutes, until well browned on all sides. Put the pan straight into the oven and roast for 7–12 minutes depending on how rare you like your meat. When cooked, transfer the lamb to a heated plate, cover and let it relax in a warm place while you make the risotto. Pour a ladleful of the stock into the pan and deglaze. Set aside.

Put the remaining stock in a saucepan and keep at a gentle simmer. Melt half the remaining butter in a large, heavy saucepan and add the shallots, celery, carrot and roasted garlic cloves. Cook gently for 10 minutes until soft, golden and translucent but not browned. Add the rice and stir until well coated with the butter and heated through. Pour in the wine and boil hard until it has reduced and almost disappeared. Add the pan juices from cooking the lamb, then begin adding the stock, a large ladleful at a time, stirring gently until each ladle has almost been absorbed by the rice. The risotto should be kept at a bare simmer throughout cooking, so don't let the rice dry out – add more stock as necessary. Continue until the rice is tender and creamy, but the grains still firm. This should take about 15–20 minutes depending on the type of rice used.

Stir in the olives and marjoram, season to taste and beat in the remaining butter. Fold in the artichokes. Cover and let rest for a couple of minutes so the risotto can relax. Carve the meat into thick slices, then serve the risotto immediately, topped with the sliced lamb.

12 fresh artichokes, prepared (see note on page 76), or 12 char-grilled deli artichokes

500 g/1 lb. lamb fillet, trimmed

1 tablespoon olive oil

125 g/1 stick unsalted butter

about 1.5 litres/6 cups hot Chicken Stock (page 150), Beef or Veal Stock (page 153) or Vegetable Stock (page 149)

2 shallots, finely chopped

1 celery stalk/rib, finely chopped

1 small carrot, finely chopped

6 roasted garlic cloves (see Roasted Garlic Risotto with Goats' Cheese and Rosemary on page 68)

400 g/2 cups risotto rice

150 ml/⅔ cup fruity white wine

20 dry-cured black olives (Greek-style), pitted

1 tablespoon finely chopped fresh marjoram

sea salt and freshly ground black pepper

SERVES 4

fennel sausage risotto

risotto di salsicce al finocchio

Italian sausages are pure minced pork – nothing added except salt and pepper and maybe chilli/
chile or fennel seeds. In Italy, you choose your cut of pork and the sausages are made in moments
right in front of you, leaving you to choose your personal seasoning preference. Tuscans like their
sausages flavoured boldly with fennel seeds and plenty of freshly ground black pepper.

Put the stock in a saucepan on the stove and keep at a gentle simmer. Melt
half the butter in a large, heavy-based saucepan then add the sausage.
Cook over a medium heat for 3–4 minutes, squashing it with a spoon to
break it up. Add the onion and garlic and cook gently for 10 minutes until
the onion is soft and golden. Add the passata, fennel seeds and thyme and
simmer for 5–10 minutes. Stir in the rice making sure it is heated through.

Begin to add the stock a large ladleful at a time, stirring gently until each
ladleful is almost absorbed into the rice. The risotto should be kept at a
bare simmer throughout cooking, so do not let the rice dry out – add more
stock as necessary. Continue until the rice is tender and creamy, but the
grains still firm. This should take between 15–20 minutes depending on
the type of rice used – look at the manufacturer's instructions.

Taste and season well with salt and pepper and beat in the remaining
butter and the Parmesan. Cover and rest for a couple of minutes to allow
the risotto to relax and the cheese to melt. You may like to add a little more
hot stock just before you serve to loosen it, but don't let the risotto hang
around too long or the rice will turn mushy. Serve in warm bowls, sprinkled
with Parmesan and garnished with thyme sprigs, if liked.

about 1.5 litres/6 cups hot Chicken
Stock (page 150) or Vegetable Stock
(page 149)

125 g/1 stick butter

450 g/1 lb. fresh Italian fennel
sausages, skins removed

1 onion, finely chopped

2 garlic cloves, finely chopped

150 ml/²⁄₃ cup passata (Italian
sieved/strained tomatoes)

1 tablespoon fresh thyme

1 tablespoon fennel seeds

500 g/2⅓ cups risotto rice, preferably
arborio or carnaroli

75 g/¾ cup freshly grated Parmesan,
plus extra to serve

sea salt and freshly ground black
pepper

thyme sprigs, to garnish (optional)

SERVES 6

italian sausage risotto with roasted onions

risotto con salsicce e cipolle arrostite

Italian sausages are pure pork – with nothing added except seasoning and maybe chilli or fennel seeds. They have a much better flavour than ordinary sausages, so it's worth seeking out a good Italian deli that stocks them in your local area.

about 1.5 litres/6 cups hot Chicken Stock (page 150) or Vegetable Stock (page 149)

125 g/1 stick unsalted butter

500 g/1 lb. fresh Italian sausages, skins removed

1 onion, finely chopped

2 garlic cloves, finely chopped

150 ml/⅔ cup passata (Italian sieved/strained tomatoes)

2 teaspoons chopped fresh thyme

500 g/2⅓ cups risotto rice

75 g/¾ cup freshly grated Parmesan, plus extra to serve

roasted onions

6 small whole red onions

100 ml/½ cup olive oil

4 tablespoons balsamic vinegar

1 tablespoon chopped fresh thyme, plus extra sprigs to serve

sea salt and freshly ground black pepper

SERVES 6

To prepare the roasted onions, preheat the oven to 200°C (400°F) Gas 6. Quarter the onions, keeping the root ends on to hold them together, then peel. Put them in a roasting pan that has been brushed with a little olive oil. Put the remaining oil, vinegar, thyme, salt and pepper in a bowl, whisk well, then brush over the onions, pouring any excess into the pan. Cover with foil and roast in the preheated oven for 15 minutes. Remove the foil and roast for a further 10 minutes, until caramelized. Keep warm.

To make the risotto, put the stock in a saucepan and keep at a gentle simmer. Melt half the butter in a large, heavy saucepan and add the sausages. Cook over medium heat for 3–4 minutes, squashing with a spoon to break them up. Add the chopped onion and garlic and cook gently for 10 minutes until the onion is soft and golden. Add the passata and thyme and simmer for 5–10 minutes. Stir in the rice, making sure it is heated through before you add the stock.

Begin adding the stock, a large ladleful at a time, stirring gently until each ladle has almost been absorbed by the rice. The risotto should be kept at a bare simmer throughout cooking, so don't let the rice dry out – add more stock as necessary. Continue until the rice is tender and creamy, but the grains still firm. This should take about 15–20 minutes depending on the type of rice used.

Taste, season well and beat in the remaining butter and all the Parmesan. Cover and let rest for a couple of minutes so the risotto can relax and the cheese melt. Serve topped with the roasted onions and sprigs of thyme.

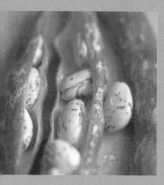

salami and borlotti bean risotto

risotto con salame e fagioli borlotti

Once the staple food of the *gente di risaia* – the workers in the rice fields of Piemonte – this comforting and fulfilling risotto is a fantastic way to use any fresh beans in season. If you can't find fresh beans, use canned beans instead, and stir them in 5 minutes from the end of cooking time just to heat them through. Sometimes a glass of local Barolo would be added to the rice before the stock is added.

Put the stock in a saucepan and keep at a gentle simmer. If using fresh beans, shell them and cook in the stock for about 20 minutes or until tender. Lift out with a slotted spoon and set aside.

Melt half the butter in a large, heavy saucepan and add the onion. Cook gently for 10 minutes until soft, golden and translucent but not browned. Stir in the salami and cook for 2 minutes. It must not brown. Add the rice and stir until well coated with the butter and heated through. Begin adding the stock, a large ladleful at a time, stirring gently until each ladle has almost been absorbed by the rice. The risotto should be kept at a bare simmer throughout cooking, so don't let the rice dry out – add more stock as necessary. Continue until the rice is tender and creamy, but the grains still firm. This should take about 15–20 minutes depending on the type of rice used. Stir in the beans just before the risotto is ready.

Taste, season well and beat in the remaining butter and all the Parmesan. Cover and let rest for a couple of minutes so the risotto can relax, then serve immediately. Serve with extra grated Parmesan.

about 1.5 litres/6 cups hot Beef or Veal Stock (page 153)

1 kg/2 lbs. fresh borlotti beans (or similar) in the pod, shelled weight of 500 g/1lb.

125 g/1 stick unsalted butter

1 onion, finely chopped

150-g/6-oz. chunk of salami, diced

400 g/2 cups risotto rice, preferably carnaroli

75 g/¾ cup freshly grated Parmesan, plus extra to serve

sea salt and freshly ground black pepper

SERVES 6

ham and leek risotto

risotto con pancetta e porri

The leek is one of my favourite vegetables – it's not used enough in my opinion. Its sweet, delicate onion flavour is an excellent complement to salty cooked ham. Try to find ham sold in the piece so you can tear it into shreds – it will be more succulent than sliced ham. Roasting garlic softens and mellows the flavour until it is almost nutty.

6 large garlic cloves

about 200 ml/¾ cup olive oil

500 g/1lb. leeks, plus 2 whole leeks to serve

vegetable oil, for deep frying

about 1.5 litres/6 cups hot Chicken Stock (page 150)

500 g/2⅓ cups risotto rice

1 tablespoon grainy mustard

350 g/12 oz. cold ham, shredded

50 g/½ cup freshly grated Parmesan

sea salt and freshly ground black pepper

SERVES 4–6

Peel the garlic cloves and put them in a small saucepan. Cover with olive oil and heat to simmering. Simmer for about 20 minutes or until the garlic is golden and soft. Let cool in the oil.

Meanwhile make the fried leeks. Cut the 2 whole leeks into 7-cm/3-inch lengths, then slice in half lengthwise and cut into long, thin shreds. Fill a wok or large saucepan one-third full with the vegetable oil and heat to 175°C (350°F), add the shredded leeks and deep-fry for 1 minute until crisp and just golden. Lift out of the oil and drain on paper towels.

Slice the remaining leeks (thinly or thickly, as you like) into rounds. Put the stock in a saucepan and keep at a gentle simmer. Heat 75 ml/⅓ cup of the garlic-flavoured olive oil in a large, heavy saucepan. Add the leeks and sauté for a few minutes until beginning to soften and colour slightly, then stir in the garlic cloves. Pour in the rice and stir until well coated with oil and heated through.

Begin to add the simmering stock, a large ladleful at a time, stirring until each ladle has been absorbed by the rice. Continue until the rice is tender and creamy, but the grains still firm. Stir in the mustard and ham. Season well, stir in the Parmesan, cover and let rest for a couple of minutes so the risotto can relax, before serving topped with a mound of crispy fried leeks.

saffron risotto with parmesan, sage and ham

risotto alla zafferano con parmigiano, salvia e prosciutto

A good risotto depends on good ingredients, so make sure you have a well-flavoured stock, good-quality ham and well-aged Parmesan (or Grana Padano) cheese.

600 ml/2½ cups chicken stock, preferably home-made

40 g/3 tablespoons butter

1 small onion or ½ medium onion, finely chopped

175 g/1 cup arborio or other Italian risotto rice

75 ml/5 tablespoons dry white wine

a Parmesan rind (optional)

a small pinch (about ¼ teaspoon) saffron strands

1–2 tablespoons jellied meat juices* (optional)

25 g/1 oz. aged Parmesan, freshly grated, plus a few Parmesan shavings

2 tablespoons olive oil

2–3 slices of prosciutto or Serrano ham, each torn into 3 pieces

8–10 fresh sage leaves

sea salt and freshly ground black pepper

SERVES 2

Bring the stock to the boil, then leave it simmering on a low heat.

Melt half the butter over medium heat in a large saucepan, add the onion and cook gently until soft, about 5 minutes. Tip in the rice, stir and cook for 2–3 minutes until the grains have turned opaque and are beginning to catch on the bottom of the pan. Add the wine, stir and let it bubble up and evaporate.

Add the Parmesan rind if you have one, then begin to add the hot stock, adding about a coffee cup at a time and allowing the liquid to be absorbed by the rice before you add the next lot. Cook, stirring regularly, until the rice begins to look creamy but still has some bite to it, about 20 minutes. Pour the last bit of stock over the saffron and add to the risotto along with a couple of spoonfuls of jellied meat juices, if you have some. Turn off the heat, add the remaining butter and the grated Parmesan and stir. Cover the pan and let the flavours amalgamate for 2–3 minutes.

Heat the oil in a frying pan/skillet and quickly fry the ham. Remove from the pan with a slotted spoon and drain on a piece of kitchen paper. Fry the sage leaves in the same pan until crisp. Give the risotto a final stir, remove the Parmesan rind and season to taste. Serve in warm, shallow soup bowls and top with the crisp ham, sage leaves and a few shavings of Parmesan.

* What you want are the umami-rich meat juices which collect under the fat you pour off when you're cooking a chicken or a pork or veal joint.

risotto with chianti, mushrooms and pancetta
risotto al chianti, funghi e pancetta

Risotto made with red wine is a miracle of flavour combinations. The sweetness from the mushrooms and cheese and the smoky saltiness from the pancetta make this especially unforgettable. The important thing to remember is to reduce the wine completely to boil off the alcohol and reduce the acidity. This is a risotto to make in the colder months, when you need big, comforting flavours. Don't let the risotto overcook and become stodgy.

Put the stock in a saucepan and keep it at a gentle simmer. Heat half the oil or butter in a large saucepan and add the chopped pancetta, cook until the fat begins to run, then add the onion and mushrooms. Cook gently for 5 minutes until softened and translucent.

Stir in the rice and cook for 1–2 minutes until the rice smells toasted and looks opaque. Add the wine and boil hard until the liquid disappears.

Begin adding the stock, a large ladleful at a time, stirring gently until each ladle has been almost absorbed by the rice. Continue until the rice is tender and creamy, but the grains still firm. Stir in the remaining olive oil and all the Parmesan. Taste and season well.

Let stand with the lid on for 5 minutes. Transfer to a large, warmed bowl and sprinkle with flat-leaf parsley. Top with the fried porcini, if using, and serve immediately.

about 1.5 litres/6 cups hot Chicken Stock (page 150) or Beef or Veal Stock (page 153)

4 tablespoons olive oil or 75 g/5 tablespoons unsalted butter

75 g/3 oz. pancetta, finely chopped

1 red onion, finely chopped

200 g/8 oz. large dark (cremini) mushrooms or porcini, finely chopped

500 g/2⅓ cups risotto rice, such as arborio

250 ml/1 cup good Chianti wine

100 g/1 cup freshly grated Parmesan

sea salt and freshly ground black pepper

to serve

2 tablespoons chopped fresh flat-leaf parsley

1 porcini, sliced and pan-fried in olive oil until golden (optional)

SERVES 6

FISH & SEAFOOD

caper risotto with grilled tuna and salmoriglio sauce

risotto con capperi, tonno e salmoriglio

The slightly musky flavour of capers is delicious in a fish risotto, especially if they are the more pungent salted ones. Served with this vibrant sauce from Sicily, it is perfect for a summer meal.

4 tuna steaks, cut 2.5 cm/1 inch thick

6 tablespoons extra virgin olive oil

sea salt and freshly ground
black pepper

salmoriglio sauce

finely grated zest and juice of
½ large unwaxed lemon, or to taste

a pinch of sugar

4 tablespoons extra virgin olive oil

1 garlic clove, finely chopped

2 teaspoons dried oregano

2 tablespoons fresh mint, finely
chopped

caper risotto

about 1.5 litres/6 cups hot Fish Stock
(page 154) or Vegetable Stock
(page 149)

1 onion, finely chopped

500 g/2⅓ cups risotto rice

150 ml/⅔ cup dry white wine

4 tablespoons capers in salt, rinsed
and then soaked for 10 minutes in
warm water

finely grated zest and juice of
1 unwaxed lemon, to taste

SERVES 4

To make the *salmoriglio* sauce, put the lemon juice and sugar in a bowl, stir to dissolve, then add the lemon zest. Whisk in the 4 tablespoons olive oil, then stir in the garlic, oregano and chopped mint. Set aside to infuse.

Preheat the grill/broiler. Brush the tuna with 2 tablespoons olive oil and season. Set on a rack in a foil-lined grill pan. Grill/broil for 1–2 minutes on each side until crusty on the outside and still pink in the middle. Remove from the heat, cover and keep it warm while you make the risotto.

Put the stock in a saucepan and keep at a gentle simmer. Heat 4 tablespoons olive oil in a large, heavy saucepan and add the onion. Cook gently for 10 minutes until soft, golden and translucent but not browned. Add the rice and stir until well coated with the oil and heated through. Add the wine and boil hard until it has reduced and almost disappeared.

Begin adding the stock, a large ladleful at a time, stirring gently until each ladle has almost been absorbed by the rice. The risotto should be kept at a bare simmer throughout cooking, so don't let the rice dry out – add more stock as necessary. Continue until the rice is tender and creamy, but the grains still firm. This should take about 15–20 minutes depending on the type of rice used.

Taste, season well and add capers, lemon juice and zest to taste. Cover and let rest for a couple of minutes so the risotto can relax. Slice the tuna steaks and arrange on top of each serving, spoon the sauce over the top and serve immediately.

smoked salmon risotto

risotto cremoso con salmone affumicato

Smoked salmon has become fashionable in Italy and I have even seen it on pizzas – overcooked and not very pleasant. However, smoked salmon is sublime in a very creamy risotto enriched with butter, cream and Parmesan (one of the few times it is respectable to use Parmesan in a fish or seafood risotto). The consistency of this risotto should be quite liquid.

Put the stock in a saucepan and keep at a gentle simmer. Melt half the butter in a large, heavy saucepan and add the shallots and garlic. Cook gently for 10 minutes until soft, golden and translucent but not browned. Add the rice and stir until well coated with the butter and heated through. Pour in the vermouth and boil hard until it has reduced and almost disappeared. This will remove the taste of raw alcohol.

Begin adding the stock, a large ladleful at a time, stirring gently until each ladle has almost been absorbed by the rice. The risotto should be kept at a bare simmer throughout cooking, so don't let the rice dry out – add more stock as necessary. Continue until the rice is tender and creamy, but the grains still firm. This should take about 15–20 minutes depending on the type of rice used.

Taste, season well and beat in the remaining butter, the cream and Parmesan. Gently fold in half the salmon, and all the dill and lemon zest. Cover and let rest for a couple of minutes so the risotto can relax and the flavours develop. Taste again and season with lemon juice, then top with the remaining smoked salmon and serve immediately.

about 1.5 litres/6 cups hot Fish Stock (page 154) or Vegetable Stock (page 149)

125 g/1 stick unsalted butter

3 shallots, very finely chopped

1 garlic clove, finely chopped

300 g/1½ cups risotto rice

75 ml/⅓ cup dry vermouth

4 tablespoons double/heavy cream or 2 tablespoons mascarpone cheese

50 g/½ cup finely grated Parmesan, plus extra to serve

200 g/7 oz. sliced smoked salmon, cut into thin strips

2 tablespoons chopped fresh dill

finely grated zest and juice of 1 unwaxed lemon

sea salt and freshly ground black pepper

SERVES 4

seafood and saffron risotto

risotto ai frutti di mare

Central and northern Italy are the places to go for good risotto – I've never eaten a really good one in the south. Seafood risotto should be creamy and slightly soupy – *all'onda*, meaning 'like a wave'. The best seafood *risotti* come from the Venice area, where seafood is abundant in the lagoons. Saffron gives a wonderful warm colour and musky flavour.

1 teaspoon saffron threads

1.5 litres/6 cups Fish Stock (page 154)

300 ml/1⅓ cups dry white wine

350 g/12 oz. uncooked prawns/shrimp tails, unpeeled

6 baby squid, cleaned and cut into rings

6 fresh scallops, halved horizontally if large

500 g/1 lb. fresh mussels, cleaned

250 g/8 oz. fresh baby/cherrystone clams (vongole) or cockles, rinsed

3 tablespoons olive oil

1 onion, finely chopped

500 g/2⅓ cups risotto rice

sea salt and freshly ground black pepper

3 tablespoons chopped fresh flat-leaf parsley, to serve

SERVES 6

Put the saffron in a small bowl and cover with boiling water. Set aside to infuse while you cook the fish.

Pour the stock and wine into a saucepan and heat to simmering point. Add the prawns/shrimp and cook for 2 minutes. Add the squid and scallops and cook for a further 2 minutes. Transfer them to a plate with a slotted spoon and set aside.

Put the mussels and clams into the stock and bring to the boil. Cover and cook for 3–5 minutes or until all the shells have opened. Transfer to a plate with a slotted spoon and set aside. Keep the stock hot.

Heat the oil in a large saucepan and add the onion. Cook gently for 5 minutes until softened and translucent. Stir in the rice and cook for 1–2 minutes until the rice smells toasted and looks opaque. Add the saffron water and begin adding the stock, a large ladleful at a time, stirring gently until each ladle has almost been absorbed by the rice. The risotto should be kept at a bare simmer throughout cooking, so don't let the rice dry out – add more stock as necessary. Continue until the rice is tender and creamy, but the grains still firm. This should take about 15–20 minutes depending on the type of rice used.

Stir in the seafood and let stand with the lid on for 5 minutes. Transfer to a large warmed bowl and sprinkle with parsley. Serve immediately.

crab and chilli risotto
risotto al granchio e peperoncino

Crab makes a delicious risotto, especially when speckled with red chilli. Although fresh crab is preferable, it's a bit fiddly to prepare and fishmongers sell frozen white and dark crabmeat which is very acceptable for this recipe. I like to stir in the creamy dark meat at the end, but this may not be to all tastes. Serve topped with crab claws for a dramatic and tasty garnish.

Put the stock in a saucepan and keep at a gentle simmer. Melt half the butter in a large, heavy saucepan and add the shallots and celery. Cook gently for 5–7 minutes until soft and golden but not browned. Add the rice, chilli and bay leaf, stir until well coated with the butter, translucent and heated through. Pour in the wine and boil hard until it has reduced and almost disappeared. This will remove the taste of raw alcohol.

Begin adding the stock, a large ladleful at a time, stirring gently until each ladle has almost been absorbed by the rice. The risotto should be kept at a bare simmer throughout cooking, so don't let the rice dry out – add more stock as necessary. Continue until the rice is tender and creamy, but the grains still firm. This should take 15–20 minutes depending on the type of rice used.

About 5 minutes before the rice is ready, stir in half the crabmeat. When the rice is cooked, taste, season well and stir in the remaining butter. Remove the bay leaf. Fold in the remaining crabmeat, being careful not to break up any lumps. Cover and let rest for a couple of minutes so the risotto can relax, then serve immediately, topped with the crab claws and lots of chopped flat-leaf parsley.

about 1.5 litres/6 cups hot Seafood Stock (page 154), Fish Stock (page 154) or Vegetable Stock (page 149)

100 g/7 tablespoons unsalted butter

3 shallots, finely chopped

2 celery stalks/ribs, finely chopped

400 g/2 cups risotto rice

1 fresh red chilli, deseeded and finely chopped

1 bay leaf

150 ml/⅔ cup dry white wine

250 g/8 oz. fresh white crabmeat (or frozen and thawed)

sea salt and freshly ground black pepper

to serve

4–8 crab claws, cooked and cracked

4 tablespoons chopped fresh flat-leaf parsley

SERVES 4

black risotto

risotto al nero di seppie

This is one of my favourite risottos – I love the rich iodine taste of the ink. Cleaned squid is available from most fishmongers. The all-important ink sacs have been packaged into little plastic sachets – find them in the chiller cabinets at fishmongers and some delis.

600 g/1lb. 5 oz. cleaned squid plus two sachets squid ink or 900 g/2 lbs. whole cuttlefish (see below)

3 tablespoons extra virgin olive oil

½ onion, finely chopped

1 garlic clove, finely chopped

about 1.5 litres/6 cups hot Fish Stock (page 154)

150 ml/⅔ cup dry white wine

500 g/2⅓ cups risotto rice, preferably vialone nano

50 g/4 tablespoons unsalted butter, softened

2 tablespoon grappa (optional)

3 tablespoons finely chopped fresh flat-leaf parsley

sea salt and freshly ground black pepper

SERVES 4–6

If using squid, cut body and tentacles into thin rings and small pieces. Keep some of the tentacles whole if you like. Heat the oil in a saucepan and add the onion and garlic. Cook gently for 10 minutes until soft, golden and translucent but not browned. Add the squid or cuttlefish, 2 ladlefuls of stock and the wine, then cover and cook gently for 20 minutes, until tender, adding a little more stock to the pan if necessary during cooking.

Add the rice and stir until well coated and heated through. Mix the ink with a little stock and stir into the risotto. Begin adding the stock, a large ladleful at a time, stirring gently until each ladle has almost been absorbed by the rice. The risotto should be kept at a bare simmer throughout cooking, so don't let the rice dry out – add more stock as necessary. Continue until the rice is tender and creamy but the grains still firm. This should take about 15–20 minutes depending on the type of rice used.

Taste, season well and beat in the butter and grappa, if using. Cover and let rest for a couple of minutes so the risotto can relax, then serve immediately topped with the chopped parsley.

Note To prepare fresh cuttlefish, rinse it, then pull the tentacles and head away from the body. Carefully remove the silvery ink sacs from the heads without piercing them. Cut off all the internal organs still attached to the head. Put the ink sacs in a tea strainer over a small bowl and press out the ink with the back of a spoon. Cut through the thin skin covering the bone in the body and lift the bone out. Wash everything thoroughly in cold water and cut the body and tentacles into thin rings and small squares.

white squid risotto

risotto bianco con calamari

For those who aren't brave enough to try risotto nero, made with squid ink, but still love squid, then this is for you. There is no sign of ink, just squid, garlic, wine and parsley. You can make this with fresh or frozen prepared squid. If you have the tentacles, they make a great topping – just quickly sear them on a stove-top grill pan. I sometimes fry a little extra sliced garlic and chopped red chilli in olive oil and pour this over the risotto before serving.

Put the stock in a saucepan and keep at a gentle simmer. Cut the squid into rings or small pieces and reserve the tentacles, if using. Melt half the butter in a large, heavy saucepan and add the onion or shallots and the garlic. Cook gently for 5 minutes until translucent but not browned. Add the squid, then the wine and cook gently for 5 minutes, until the squid is white and the wine beginning to disappear. Add the rice and stir until well coated with the butter, wine and squid and heated through.

Begin adding the stock, a large ladle at a time, stirring gently until each ladle has almost been absorbed by the rice. The risotto should be kept at a bare simmer throughout cooking, so don't let the rice dry out – add more stock as necessary. Continue until the rice is tender and creamy, but the grains still firm. (This should take 15–20 minutes depending on the type of rice used – check the packet instructions.)

Taste and season well with salt and pepper and beat in the remaining butter and the parsley. Cover and let rest for a couple of minutes so the risotto can relax. Meanwhile heat a stove-top grill pan to smoking hot, toss the tentacles in the olive oil to coat and add them to the pan. Cook for 1–2 minutes, then remove to a plate. Check the risotto – you may like to add a little more hot stock to the risotto just before you serve to loosen it, but don't let it wait around too long or the rice will turn mushy. Serve with the tentacles on top.

about 1.5 litres/6 cups hot Vegetable Stock (page 149) or Seafood Stock (page 154)

300 g/10½ oz. fresh or frozen prepared squid (to prepare fresh squid or cuttlefish, see page 121)

125 g/1 stick unsalted butter

1 onion or 2 shallots, finely chopped

2–3 large garlic cloves, finely chopped

75 ml/5 tablespoons dry white wine

300 g/1½ cups risotto rice, preferably carnaroli

2 tablespoons chopped fresh parsley

1–2 tablespoons olive oil

sea salt and freshly ground black pepper

SERVES 4

lobster or shrimp risotto

risotto all'aragosta o gamberi

This is a quick way to cook a special risotto. If making this with prawns/shrimp cook them first, peel them, then pound the shells and add to the stock for extra flavour. Add the chopped prawns/shrimp where you would the lobster flesh.

Put the stock in a saucepan and keep at a gentle simmer. Split the lobsters in half and remove the stomach sac and long intestine. Prise out the tail meat and any red coral or roe and set aside. Crack the claws and extract the meat and set aside. Put all the shells including the heads into a solid bowl and pound them with the end of a rolling pin until they are broken into small fragments. Add these to the stock and simmer for 30 minutes. Cut the lobster meat into chunks and chop up the roe. Strain the stock and return to the heat. Discard the contents of the sieve/strainer.

Melt half the butter in a large, heavy saucepan and add the shallots. Cook gently for 5 minutes until soft, golden and translucent but not browned. Add the rice and stir until well coated with the butter and heated through. Pour in the vermouth and boil hard until it has reduced and almost disappeared. This will remove the taste of raw alcohol.

Begin adding the stock, a large ladleful at a time, stirring gently until each ladle has almost been absorbed by the rice. The risotto should be kept at a bare simmer throughout cooking, so don't let the rice dry out – add more stock as necessary. Continue until the rice is tender and creamy, but the grains still firm. This should take about 15–20 minutes depending on the type of rice used.

Taste, season well with salt, pepper and lemon juice, beat in the remaining butter and reserved roe and gently fold in the lobster meat. Cover and let rest for a couple of minutes so the risotto can relax and the lobster heat through, then serve immediately. Serve sprinkled with a little cayenne.

about 1.5 litres/6 cups hot Seafood Stock (page 154) or Vegetable Stock (page 149)

2 medium cooked lobsters, about 500–600 g/1 lb–1lb.5 oz. each, or similar weight of prawns/shrimp

125 g/1 stick unsalted butter

2 shallots, finely chopped

500 g/2⅓ cups risotto rice

3 tablespoons sweet red vermouth

sea salt and freshly ground black pepper

freshly squeezed lemon juice

a pinch of cayenne, to serve

SERVES 6

scallop and spring onion risotto

risotto con capesante e cipollotti

Cooking this rich risotto with dry vermouth instead of wine gives it a certain finesse and a herbal note. I often use dry vermouth when cooking fish and seafood when I don't have any wine open.

about 1.5 litres/6 cups hot Seafood Stock (page 154), Fish Stock (page 154) or Vegetable Stock (page 149)

12 large fresh or frozen scallops (with or without orange roes or coral)

125 g/1 stick unsalted butter

6 spring onions/scallions, sliced or chopped (white and green parts kept separate)

400 g/2 cups risotto rice, preferably carnaroli

75 ml/⅓ cup dry white vermouth

sea salt and freshly ground black pepper

SERVES 4

Put the stock in a saucepan and keep at a gentle simmer. Look at the scallops and check to see if there is a tiny tough white muscle clinging to the side – if there is, pull off and discard. Separate the corals or roes from the white meat. Slice each scallop in half around the middle. Set aside. Melt half the butter in a large, heavy saucepan and, when foaming, fry the scallops quickly, browning them on both sides. Remove to a plate before they overcook: they will only take 2 minutes at the most. Add the white part of the spring onion/scallion and cook gently for 3–4 minutes until soft, golden and translucent but not browned.

Add the rice and stir until well coated with the butter and heated through. Pour in the vermouth and boil hard until it has reduced and almost disappeared. This will remove the taste of raw alcohol.

Begin adding the stock, a large ladleful at a time, stirring gently until each ladle has almost been absorbed by the rice. The risotto should be kept at a bare simmer throughout cooking, so don't let the rice dry out – add more stock as necessary. Continue until the rice is tender and creamy, but the grains still firm. This should take about 15–20 minutes depending on the type of rice used.

Taste, season well and beat in the remaining butter and fold in the scallops and green parts of the spring onions/scallions. Cover and let rest for a couple of minutes so the risotto can relax and the scallops heat through, then serve immediately. You may like to add a little more hot stock to the risotto just before you serve to loosen it, but don't let it wait around too long or the rice will turn mushy and the scallops will overcook.

smoked mussel or oyster and leek risotto

risotto con cozze o ostriche affumicate

Though it still tastes luxurious, the ingredients for this risotto are ordinary storecupboard basics. Canned smoked fish is a wonderful standby – for extra flavour, keep the oil and use it instead of the butter for softening the vegetables. A hint of tarragon is always good with smoky things, as is the sweetness of the leeks. This would also work well with flakes of any smoked fish such as mackerel or Scottish 'smokies' (smoked haddock).

Put the stock in a saucepan and keep at a gentle simmer. Melt half the butter in a large, heavy saucepan and, when foaming, add the sliced leek and celery and cook gently for 5 minutes until softened but not browned. Add the rice and stir until well coated with the butter and heated through. Pour in the vermouth and boil hard until it has reduced and almost disappeared. This will remove the taste of raw alcohol. Add the tarragon.

Begin adding the stock, a large ladleful at a time, stirring gently until each ladle has almost been absorbed by the rice. The risotto should be kept at a bare simmer throughout cooking, so don't let the rice dry out – add more stock as necessary. Continue until the rice is tender and creamy, but the grains still firm. This should take about 15–20 minutes depending on the type of rice used.

Taste, season well and beat in the remaining butter and fold in the smoked mussels or oysters. Cover and let rest for a couple of minutes so the risotto can relax and the seafood heat through, then serve immediately.

about 1.5 litres/6 cups hot Vegetable Stock (page 149)

125 g/1 stick unsalted butter

1 large leek, finely sliced or chopped (all the white part and half of the green)

1 celery stalk/rib, finely chopped

400 g/2 cups risotto rice, preferably carnaroli

75 ml/⅓ cup dry white vermouth

1 teaspoon chopped fresh tarragon

3 cans smoked mussels or oysters, 85 g/3 oz. each, drained

sea salt and freshly ground black pepper

SERVES 4

mussel or clam risotto
risotto con cozze o vongole

Here is a simple risotto relying on the freshness and delicate flavours of the mussels or clams. When I have it, I like to add chopped fresh chervil, which gives a hint of aniseed.

1.5 kg/3 lbs. mussels or small clams

about 1.5 litres/6 cups hot Fish Stock (page 154) or Vegetable Stock (page 149)

125 g/1 stick unsalted butter

1 small onion, finely chopped

2 garlic cloves, finely chopped

500 g/2⅓ cups risotto rice, preferably vialone nano

3 tablespoons chopped fresh flat-leaf parsley

sea salt and freshly ground black pepper

SERVES 6

Discard any mussels or clams with broken shells, or any that are open and will not close when sharply tapped against a surface. Wash and scrub them thoroughly, pulling off any beards, then let soak in cold water for an hour to purge them. Drain and transfer to a large saucepan over high heat, with no extra water other than whatever is still clinging to them. Cover and steam for 2–5 minutes (2–3 for clams, 4–5 for mussels), until they open fully, giving the pan a shake now and then. Strain them through a colander and reserve the cooking liquid. When cool enough to handle, remove the flesh from the shells, leaving a few in their shells for serving. Strain the resulting liquid through a very fine sieve or muslin to remove any grit.

Put the stock in a saucepan and keep at a gentle simmer. Melt half the butter in a large, heavy saucepan and add the onion and garlic. Cook gently for 10 minutes until soft, golden and translucent but not browned. Add the rice and stir until well coated with the butter and heated through. Stir in the strained mussel liquid. When this has been absorbed, begin adding the stock, a large ladleful at a time, stirring gently until each ladle has almost been absorbed by the rice. The risotto should be kept at a bare simmer throughout cooking, so don't let the rice dry out – add more stock as necessary. Continue until the rice is tender and creamy, but the grains are still firm. This should take about 15–20 minutes depending on the type of rice you have used.

Taste, season well and beat in the remaining butter. Fold in the cooked mussels or clams and 2 tablespoons of the parsley. Cover and let rest for a few minutes so the risotto can relax and the shellfish heat through. Serve topped with the remaining parsley and the reserved mussels in their shells.

OTHER WAYS WITH RISOTTO

rice croquettes with tomato sauce

supp\`i al telefono con sugo di pomodoro

Suppl\`i* are real comfort food. When you bite one, you can pull the melted oozing mozzarella into strings that are said to look like telephone wires strung from pole to pole – hence the name, *suppl\`i al telefono. You can make it with leftover risotto, but it is worth making from scratch.

tomato sauce

125 ml/½ cup olive oil

2 garlic cloves, chopped

1 teaspoon dried oregano

800 g/1 lb. 12 oz. fresh tomatoes, skinned and coarsely chopped, or two 400-g/14-oz. cans chopped tomatoes

sea salt and freshly ground black pepper

suppl\`i

2 eggs, lightly beaten

⅓ recipe Parmesan and Butter Risotto (see page 21)

115 g/4 oz. mozzarella cheese, cut into 20 cubes

2 slices of cooked ham or mortadella, cut into 20 strips

100 g/⅔ cup dried white breadcrumbs, for coating

sea salt and freshly ground black pepper

vegetable oil, for deep frying

MAKES 20

First make the tomato sauce, heat the oil almost to smoking point in a large shallow pan or wok. Standing back (it will splutter if it's at the right temperature), add the garlic, oregano, tomatoes and pepper. To acquire its distinctive, concentrated, almost caramelized flavour, the tomatoes must fry at a very lively heat in a shallow pan, so cook over fierce heat for 5–8 minutes or until the sauce is thick and glossy. Add salt to taste, pass through a food mill or blend in a food processor, then sieve/strain to remove the seeds. Set aside.

Beat the eggs into the risotto. Spread the mixture out on a plate and let cool completely, about 1 hour.

Take a large spoonful of risotto and, with damp hands, mould it into an egg shape. Insert your little finger down through the top of the egg but not quite to the bottom, to make a hole inside. Push in a cube of cheese wrapped with a strip of ham and pinch the top over to seal. Roll the egg shape into a fat cylinder, making sure the filling doesn't burst through. Set on a tray while you make the others. Put the breadcrumbs in a shallow bowl. Roll the suppl\`i in the breadcrumbs until evenly coated. At this stage they can be covered and left in the refrigerator for up to 1 day.

Heat the oil in a large saucepan until a crumb will sizzle immediately – 180°C (350°F). Fry 3–4 at a time for 4–5 minutes until deep golden. Drain on paper towels, sprinkle with salt and serve immediately with warm tomato sauce (or keep warm in a low oven for up to 15 minutes).

little tomato risotto cakes
saltimbocca di risotto

Beware, these irresistible little, cocktail-sized mouthfuls will mysteriously jump into your mouth as you cook them. After they are completely assembled, they can be refrigerated for up to a day, ready to fry at the last moment. They will keep warm in a low oven for 30 minutes — but keep them covered and don't add a topping until the last minute.

Put the stock and tomato or vegetable juice in a saucepan and keep at a gentle simmer. Heat the olive oil in a large, heavy saucepan and add the onion. Cook gently for 5 minutes, then add the garlic and cook for a further 5 minutes until soft, golden and translucent but not browned. Add the rice, then stir until well coated with the oil and heated through. Pour in the wine and boil hard until it has reduced and almost disappeared. Stir in the sun-dried tomato paste.

Add the stock, a large ladleful at a time, stirring gently until each ladle has almost been absorbed by the rice. The risotto should be kept at a bare simmer throughout cooking, so don't let the rice dry out — add more stock as necessary. Continue until the rice is tender and creamy, and thicker than normal. This should take about 20 minutes depending on the type of rice used. Stir in the sun-blushed tomatoes and Parmesan.

Taste, season well and beat in the egg. Spread out the mixture on a tray until cool enough to handle, about 30 minutes. Roll into bite-sized balls with damp hands, flatten, set on a tray and cover with clingfilm/plastic wrap. Leave to firm up in the refrigerator. When firm, put a basil leaf on top of each one and wrap with a strip of pancetta. Heat a little oil in a non-stick frying pan/skillet and fry for about 1 minute on each side until golden. Serve warm as a snack with drinks.

500 ml/2 cups hot Vegetable Stock (page 149)

500 ml/2 cups tomato juice or mixed vegetable juice, such as V8

3 tablespoons olive oil

1 small onion, finely chopped

1 garlic clove, finely chopped

225 g/1 heaping cup risotto rice, preferably arborio

150 ml/⅔ cup dry white wine

4 tablespoons sun-dried tomato paste

125 g/5 oz. sun-blushed tomatoes, chopped

50 g/½ cup freshly grated Parmesan

1 small egg, beaten

32 fresh basil leaves, plus extra to serve

16 paper thin slices of pancetta, halved

sea salt and freshly ground black pepper

MAKES ABOUT 32

sicilian fried rice balls

arancini di riso di siciliane

These crisp golden balls, stuffed with leftover meat ragù, are eaten as street food in Sicily. However, when made cocktail snack size, they are the perfect hot nibble to serve with drinks.

75 g/6 tablespoons unsalted butter

1 onion, finely chopped

150 ml/⅔ cup dry white wine

275 g/1⅓ cups risotto rice, preferably arborio

900 ml/3⅔ cups hot Vegetable Stock (page 149) or Chicken Stock (page 150)

8 saffron threads or ¼ teaspoon powdered saffron

25 g/¼ cup freshly grated Parmesan

1 small egg

about 250 g/1 cup meat sauce (see page 93), or use leftover ragù

sea salt and freshly ground black pepper

vegetable oil, for deep-frying

coating

100 g/⅔ cup plain/all-purpose flour

2 large eggs, beaten

125 g/¾ cup dried white breadcrumbs

an electric deep-fryer or wok

SERVES 4–6

Melt the butter in a large, heavy saucepan and add the onion. Cook gently for 10 minutes until soft and golden but not browned. Pour in the wine and boil hard until reduced and almost disappeared. Stir in the rice and coat with the butter and wine. Add a ladleful of stock and the saffron and simmer, stirring until absorbed. Continue adding the stock, ladle by ladle, until all the stock has been absorbed. The rice should be very tender, thick and golden. This should take about 20 minutes.

Taste, season well and stir in the Parmesan. Lightly whisk the egg and beat into the risotto. Spread out on a plate and let cool completely, about 1 hour. Take 1 tablespoon cold risotto and, with damp hands, spread out in the palm of one hand. Mound a small teaspoon of meat ragù in the centre. Take another tablespoon of risotto and set over the ragù to enclose it completely. Carefully roll and smooth in your hands to form a perfect round ball. Continue until all the risotto and filling have been used.

To make the coating, put the flour on a plate, the beaten egg in a shallow dish and the breadcrumbs in a shallow bowl. Roll the balls first in the flour, then in the egg and finally roll in the breadcrumbs until coated.

Heat the oil in a deep-fryer or wok until a crumb will sizzle immediately on contact – 180°C (350°F). Fry a few balls at a time for 3–5 minutes, until deep golden. Drain on paper towels, sprinkle with salt and serve immediately (or keep warm in a low oven for up to 15 minutes).

Note For vegetarians, instead of the meat sauce filling, use 115 g/4 oz. finely chopped mozzarella, 4 sun-dried tomatoes in oil, drained and finely chopped, and a few finely chopped fresh basil leaves.

three-coloured rice and cheese cake

torta di riso e formaggio tricolore

Ideal for an indulgent lunch, this creamy rice cake oozes with mozzarella, and has pockets of tomatoes that burst with flavour. You could even add a layer of cubed mozzarella to the middle of the tart, so that the centre exudes strings of melted cheese when you cut it.

Dust the prepared cake tin/pan with the polenta or dried breadcrumbs.

If using fresh spinach, tear off the stems. Wash the leaves well, then put them, still wet, in a covered saucepan and cook for a few minutes until wilted. Drain well but do not squeeze dry – you want large pieces of spinach. If using thawed spinach, lightly squeeze it to remove excess moisture and toss the leaves a little to loosen them. Mix the spinach into the beaten eggs.

Cook the rice in a large saucepan of boiling salted water for about 10 minutes, until almost tender, then drain through a sieve. Meanwhile, heat the oil and butter in a frying pan. Add the onion and cook until golden. Stir into the rice.

Season the egg and spinach mixture with nutmeg, salt and pepper. Stir into the rice, then fold in the cherry tomatoes, cubed mozzarella and Parmesan. Spoon into the prepared cake tin/pan and level the surface.

Bake in a preheated oven at 200°C (400°F) Gas 6 for 25–30 minutes, until firm and golden. Turn out and serve hot, cut into wedges.

30 g/¼ cup polenta, cornmeal or dried breadcrumbs

500 g/1 lb. fresh or 250 g/8 oz. frozen whole leaf spinach, thawed

3 eggs, beaten

250 g/1 cup Italian risotto rice

1 tablespoon olive oil

25 g/2 tablespoons unsalted butter

1 onion, finely chopped

freshly grated nutmeg

150 g/8 oz. tiny cherry tomatoes

175 g/6 oz. mozzarella cheese, drained and cubed

4 tablespoons freshly grated Parmesan

sea salt and freshly ground black pepper

a 20-cm/8-inch non-stick springform cake tin/pan, heavily buttered

SERVES 6

cherry and almond risotto puddings

budini di riso con amarene e mandorle

This is my version of Sweet Risotto Cake (*torta di riso dolce*), so popular throughout Italy. The cooked rice is often mixed with candied fruits and nuts, but this is not to everyone's taste, so I mix in amarena cherries (a great favourite of mine), ground almonds and pistachios. Normally this is cooked in a cake tin/pan and tends to be a bit dry, so I cook them individually and serve with amarena syrup poured over the top. Amarena cherries are available in pretty blue and white glass jars or in less expensive cans.

175 g/¾ cup Italian risotto rice, preferably vialone nano

1 litre/4 cups whole milk

400 g/14 oz. canned or bottled amarena cherries, plus extra to serve

6 eggs

150 g/¾ cup caster/superfine sugar

50 g/½ cup ground almonds

grated zest of 1 unwaxed lemon

3 tablespoons maraschino liqueur or brandy

50 g/⅓ cup pistachio nuts, halved

6–8 ramekins or dariole moulds, lightly buttered, then dusted with semolina

a baking sheet

SERVES 6–8

Put the rice and the milk in a saucepan. Slowly bring to the boil, turn down the heat and simmer for 15 minutes. Drain the cherries and reserve the syrup. Halve the cherries, rinse and dry on paper towels.

Put the eggs, sugar, ground almonds, lemon zest and liqueur in a large bowl and beat until pale and creamy. Fold into the rice, then fold in the halved cherries and pistachios. Spoon into the moulds and level the tops. Set the filled moulds on the baking sheet and bake in a preheated oven at 180°C (350°F) Gas 4 for about 25 minutes or until a wooden skewer inserted in the centre comes out clean. The puddings should be set and golden brown.

Let cool in the moulds for 5 minutes, then run a knife around the edge to loosen. Invert onto serving plates. Serve warm or cold with the reserved cherry syrup and extra cherries.

Note If you have the time, grind your own almonds and the flavour will be so much better. Put the blanched almonds in the freezer for 30 minutes, then grind them in a food processor using the pulse button. This will prevent them from becoming too oily.

dark chocolate Easter risotto

riso nero di Pasqua

A delicious creamy risotto based on an ancient recipe from the north-east coast of Sicily. Chocolate arrived in Sicily from the New World via the court of Spain – the Spanish used it as a drink and a flavouring ingredient. Chocolate is still made in Modica today and is slightly grainy and not overly processed, retaining its ancient roots. It is variously flavoured with vanilla, cinnamon and chilli (a flavour beloved by Sicilians). A pinch of ground chilli in the risotto mixture here will adds a warmth and mysterious flavour – for adults only.

Put the cocoa, sugar and cinnamon in a small bowl and add 4 tablespoons of the milk. Mix until well blended, then add another 4 tablespoons milk.

Put the rice in a medium saucepan and stir in the cocoa-flavoured milk, the remaining milk and the strips of orange zest. Slowly bring to the boil, then reduce the heat, cover and barely simmer for 20 minutes. The rice should be very tender, creamy and slightly sloppy (if not, add a little extra hot milk). Remove the strips of orange zest and stir in the chocolate until it has completely melted, then the candied orange peel, if using.

Spoon into 4 small warm bowls or glass heatproof dishes and set a cinnamon stick and a slice of candied peel in each one. Sprinkle with icing/confectioners' sugar, serve immediately with pouring cream and eat while still warm.

3 tablespoons unsweetened cocoa powder

100 g/½ cup sugar

¼ teaspoon ground cinnamon

900 ml/3⅔ cup whole milk

175 g/¾ cup risotto rice, preferably vialone nano

3 long strips of orange zest

100 g/3½ oz. dark/bittersweet chocolate, grated

75 g/½ cup chopped candied orange peel (optional)

to serve

cinnamon sticks

candied orange peel

icing/confectioners' sugar

single/light cream

SERVES 4

BASIC STOCKS

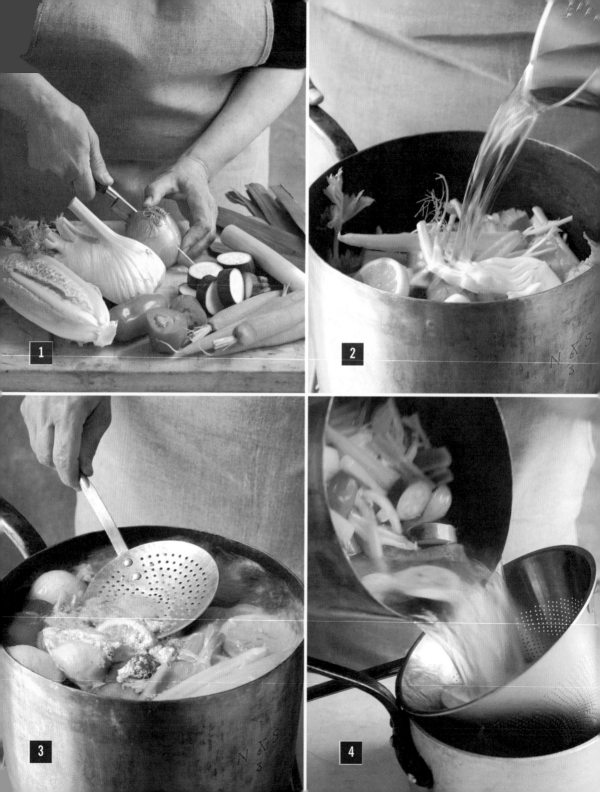

vegetable stock
brodo vegetale

Too many vegetable stocks are insipid but this stock is extravagant in its use of vegetables and has a very good flavour. Stock gives a risotto body and depth of flavour, but shouldn't dominate the dish. Strong root vegetables such as turnips and parsnips are not good additions, and neither are potatoes or cabbage. Although you should always use the best and freshest ingredients, bits and pieces lurking in the refrigerator vegetable drawer can be used.

1 large onion, quartered

4 small or 2 large carrots, quartered

1 small head of celery, coarsely chopped (including leaves)

2 leeks, white parts only, halved lengthwise, rinsed and halved again

4 courgettes/zucchini, thickly sliced

2 tomatoes, halved around the middle and seeds squeezed out

1 fennel bulb, quartered

1 cos lettuce heart, coarsely chopped

3 garlic cloves

1 dried red chilli

4 fresh bay leaves

a handful of parsley stalks, crushed

½ an unwaxed lemon, sliced

6 black peppercorns

sea salt, to taste

MAKES 2–3 LITRES/QUARTS

(1) Prepare the vegetables, washing them thoroughly before use or else your stock will be gritty.

(2) Put all the ingredients into a large stockpot, and cover with about 4 litres/4 quarts cold water. Bring to the boil and simmer for 15 minutes.

(3) Stir the stock and skim, then cook at the barest simmer for 1 hour, skimming often.

(4) Remove from the heat and strain the stock into a bowl through a fine sieve/strainer or colander lined with muslin/cheesecloth. Discard the contents of the sieve after they have cooled. Cool the stock and refrigerate for several hours.

At this stage you can reboil the stock to concentrate it, or cover and chill in the refrigerator or freeze until needed.

The stock will keep in the refrigerator for 3 days or in the freezer for up to 6 months.

chicken stock
brodo di pollo

Although Italians are not shy of using stock cubes (*dadi da brodo*), a good stock is worth making and can add real depth of flavour to a risotto. It is important not to make the stock too concentrated or dark in colour – it mustn't mask the true flavours in the risotto. You can make the stock by using a whole chicken instead of chicken wings if you like, but I think this is sometimes a waste and chicken wings are flavoursome and give a good jellied stock.

(**1**) To make the bouquet garni, bundle the bay leaves, thyme, rosemary, parsley stalks and celery leaves together and tie securely with kitchen string. Set aside until needed.

(**2**) Cut the chicken wings into pieces through their joints. Put these into a large stockpot with the carrots, onions, celery and peppercorns.

(**3**) Add enough cold water to cover, about 4 litres/quarts, and add the bouquet garni. Bring to the boil. As soon as it boils, reduce the heat to a simmer, stir and skim.

(**4**) Continue to cook at the barest simmer for 3 hours, skimming often. Remove from the heat and strain the stock into a bowl through a fine sieve/strainer or a colander lined with muslin/cheesecloth.

When cool, discard the contents of the colander. Cool the stock and refrigerate for several hours. Remove from the refrigerator and lift off any fat that has set on top of the jellied stock. At this stage you can reboil the stock to concentrate it, or cover and refrigerate or freeze until needed. This stock will keep in the refrigerator for 3–4 days or in the freezer for up to 6 months.

1.5 kg/ 3½ lbs. chicken wings

2 carrots, coarsely chopped

2 onions, coarsely chopped

1 small head of celery, including any leaves, trimmed, coarsely chopped, then washed

a few black peppercorns

bouquet garni:

4 fresh bay leaves

4 sprigs of thyme

2 sprigs of rosemary

6 parsley stalks, no leaves

a few celery leaves

MAKES 2–3 LITRES/QUARTS

beef or veal stock

brodo di manzo o vitello

I like to use a light stock for making risotto, therefore I do not brown the meat, bones or vegetables before simmering. My stock has body and is well flavoured. However, if you prefer a richer stock, brown the bones in a hot oven and, while they are browning, fry the meat and vegetables in the stockpot until they are a good red-brown, but do not let them over-brown or they will give the stock a bitter taste. If you don't have access to bones (these do give a great deal of body to the stock), add the same weight of beef or veal with good amounts of connective tissue – such as you find in cheap, tough cuts.

800 g/2 lbs. shin of beef or veal or brisket

500 g/1 lb. beef or veal bones

1 onion, coarsely chopped

2 carrots, coarsely chopped

2 leeks, split, washed and chopped

2 celery stalks/ribs, coarsely chopped

a few parsley stalks, lightly crushed

2 bay leaves

6 whole black peppercorns

a pinch of sea salt

MAKES 2–3 LITRES/QUARTS

Put all the ingredients in a large stockpot. Add enough water to cover, about 4 litres/quarts, and bring to the boil. As soon as it boils, reduce the heat to simmering, stir and skim the surface, then continue to cook at the barest simmer for 3 hours, skimming often.

Remove from the heat and strain the stock into a bowl through a fine sieve/strainer or a colander lined with muslin/cheesecloth. Discard the contents after they have cooled. Cool the stock, then refrigerate for several hours. Remove from the refrigerator and lift off any fat that has set on top of the jellied stock.

At this stage you can reboil the stock to concentrate it, or cover and refrigerate or freeze until needed. This stock will keep in the refrigerator for about 3–4 days or in the freezer for up to 6 months.

Variation Game Stock with Wild Boar or Venison
When a recipe calls for game stock, make the recipe above, using wild boar or venison meat and bones (or veal bones), or use beef stock instead.

fish stock
brodo di pesce

Use trimmings and bones left from filleting white fish such as sole, plaice, cod or haddock. Oily fish like salmon, sardines and mackerel should be avoided as they are too strong in flavour.

1 leek, split, washed and chopped

2 celery stalks/ribs, coarsely chopped

1 carrot, coarsely chopped

a few parsley stalks, lightly crushed

2 fresh bay leaves

3 thick lemon slices

4 black peppercorns and a good pinch of salt

100 ml/½ cup dry white wine

1.5 kg/3 lbs. white fish trimmings (skin) and bones, chopped

MAKES 2–3 LITRES/QUARTS

Put all the ingredients except the fish trimmings and bones in a large stockpot. Add water to cover, about 4 litres/quarts, and bring to the boil. As soon as it boils, reduce the heat and simmer for 15 minutes. Stir, skim, then add the trimmings and bones. Slowly return to the boil, then reduce the heat and cook at the barest simmer for no more than 20 minutes, skimming often.

Remove from the heat and strain the stock into a bowl through a fine sieve/strainer or a colander lined with muslin/cheesecloth. Discard the contents when they have cooled. Cool the stock, then refrigerate for several hours.

At this stage you can reboil the stock to concentrate it, or cover and refrigerate or freeze until needed. The stock will keep in the fridge for 2 days or frozen for up to 3 months.

seafood stock
brodo di frutti di mare

This is a good way to use up any prawn/shrimp heads or shells, or crab or lobster shells you would usually throw away. This stock is quite sweet, unlike a stock made with white fish.

1 onion or ½ leek, chopped

1 celery stalk/rib with leaves, coarsely chopped

a few parsley stalks, lightly crushed

2 bay leaves

2 lemon slices

4 black peppercorns

75 ml/¼ cup dry white wine

a good pinch of salt

1 kg/2 lbs. seafood pieces (prawn/shrimp heads or cheap prawns/shrimp, crab, lobster or crawfish shells)

MAKES 2 LITRES/QUARTS

Put all the ingredients except the seafood pieces in a large stockpot. Add water to cover, about 3 litres/quarts, and bring to the boil. As soon as it boils, reduce the heat and simmer for 15 minutes. Stir the stock and skim, then add the seafood pieces. Slowly return to the boil, then reduce the heat and cook at the barest simmer for 20 minutes, skimming often.

Remove from the heat and strain the stock into a bowl through a fine sieve/strainer or a colander lined with muslin/cheesecloth. Discard the contents when they have cooled. Cool the stock, then refrigerate for several hours.

At this stage you can reboil the stock to concentrate it, or cover and refrigerate or freeze until needed. The stock will keep in the fridge for 2 days or frozen for up to 3 months.

UK useful websites

GROW YOUR OWN

www.seedsofitaly.com
Real Italian seeds supplied mail order for growing your own Italian fruit, vegetables and herbs at home.

KITCHEN EQUIPMENT

Lakeland
Tel: 015394 88100
www.lakeland.co.uk
Huge range of bakeware and cookery equipment available by mail order, online and from their shops. Phone for a catalogue.

Bartolini
Via dei Servi 72/r
50122 Florence
Italy
A fine Italian cookware shop and a temple of gastronomy. Well worth a visit if you find yourself in Florence.

The Cooks' Kitchen
Tel: 01275 842883
www.thecookskitchen.com
Mail order company with everything you could need for cooking Italian-style. You can browse by country and they even have those giant pepper mills!

www.cucinadirect.com
Good mail order kitchenware shop with specialist Italian kitchen tools available.

Divertimenti
227–229 Brompton Road
London SW3 2EP
Tel: 020 7581 8065
and
74–75 Marylebone High Street,
London W1U 5JW
Tel: 020 7467 5347
www.divertimenti.co.uk
Two London shops selling beautiful kitchenware and Italian ceramics plus a mail order service. They offer knife sharpening and a copper retinning service for saucepans.

ITALIAN FOOD

Baroni
Mercato Centrale
Florence
Italy
www.baronialimentari.it
The Baroni family offers top-quality condiments, oils, aged balsamic vinagars, fresh alpine butter, fresh black and white truffles in season and truffle products and will ship all over the world. Visit when in Florence, or browse the website to be transported.

Carluccio's
www.carluccios.com
Italian caffès nationwide selling quality Italian produce, cured goods, pasta, grains and condiments.

Esperya
www.esperya.com
Genuine, high-quality foods from all regions of Italy (olive oil, wine, honey, pasta, rice, puddings, charcuterie, cheeses, preserves and seafood). UK and US websites available.

Fratelli Camisa
Unit 4, I.O.Centre
Lea Road, Waltham Cross
Hertfordshire EN9 1AS
Tel: 01992 763076
www.camisa.co.uk
Fratelli Camisa is an online deli with an incredible array of food, books and hard-to-find kitchen equipment.

www.italianwinereview.com
Interesting and impartial news and information about Italian wines.

The Oil Merchant Ltd
5 Goldhawk Mews
London W12 8PA
Tel: 020 8740 1335
www.oilmerchant.co.uk
Italian olive oils and dressings, vinegar, pesto and other sauces. Mail order, retail and wholesale.

Olives Direct
Units 8/9
Williams Industrial Park
New Milton
Hampshire BH25 6SH
Tel: 01425 613000
www.olivesdirect.co.uk
Selection of the finest quality fresh olives available by mail order. Website offers nearly 30 varieties, as well as sun-dried tomatoes.

Valvona & Crolla
19 Elm Row,
Edinburgh EH7 4AA
Tel: 0131 556 6066
www.valvonacrolla.co.uk
Edinburgh-based Italian deli selling a wide range of products, including cured meats, oils, wines and condiments.

Sapori d'Italia
Sapori House
Unit 1 & 2
Travellers Lane – Welham Green
Hatfield AL9 7HB
Tel: 01707 261800
www.saporiuk.com
Italian olive oil and dressings, pesto and other sauces, pasta, vinegar, marinated grilled vegetables and much morer. Visit the cafe or see their website for details of their mail order service.

The Italian Trade Commission
14 Waterloo Place
Westminster
London SW1Y 4AR
Tel: 020 7389 0300
www.italtrade.com
The UK official site of the foods and wines of Italy. Includes advice on how to eat Italian-style, plus the fascinating history and lore of Italy's food and wine.

US useful websites

GROW YOUR OWN

The Cook's Garden
PO Box C5030
Warminster, PA 18974
Tel: 800 457 9703
www.cooksgarden.com
An excellent resource for the kitchen gardener. Choose from a wide variety of seeds for Italian-style produce.

KITCHEN EQUIPMENT

Williams-Sonoma
Tel: 877 812 6235
www.williams-sonoma.com
A wide range of cookware and kitchen equipment, available mail order or at stores nationwide.

Bed Bath & Beyond
Tel: 800 462 3966
www.bedbathandbeyond.com
Basic kitchen equipment available to order online from stores nationwide.

Bridge Kitchenware
198-B Mount Pleasant Avenue
East Hanover, NJ 07936
Tel: (973)884-9000
www.bridgekitchenware.com
Imported European kitchenware for home and professional chefs.

Chef's Catalog
www.chefscatalog.com
Top suppliers of kitchen equipment, including Italian classic brands such as De'Longhi, available by mail order.

Crate & Barrel
Tel: 800 967 6696
www.crateandbarrel.com
Wide range of cookware and kitchen tools, available to order online of at stores nationalwide.

Sur la Table
PO Box 840
Brownsburg, IN 46112
Tel: 800 243 0852
www.surlatable.com
Elegant Italian cookware and linens.

ITALIAN FOOD

Baroni
Mercato Centrale
Florence
Italy
www.baronialimentari.it
The Baroni family offers top-quality condiments, oils, aged balsamic vinegars, fresh alpine butter, fresh black and white truffles in season, and truffle products and will ship to the US.

ChefShop.com
PO BOX 3488
Seattle, WA 98114
Tel: 800 596 0885
www.chefshop.com
Features a wide range of quality Italian ingredients, including Arborio rice, plus authentic condiments and seasonings.

Dean and DeLuca
2526 E 36th Circle North
Wichita, KS 67219
Tel: 800 221 7714
www.deandeluca.com
Gourmet gifts, fine foods, wine and kitchenware available online from this legendary Italian deli.

Gambero Rosso
www.gamberorosso.it
Fascinating Italian gastronomic website featuring information on books, food, wine, local events and more.

Wine-Searcher
www.wine-searcher.com
Invaluable search engine for finding local importers of Italian wines in the US.

Penzeys Spices
Tel: 800 741 7787
www.penzeys.com
Penzeys Spice offers more than 250 herbs, spices, and seasonings, including many suitable for use in risottos. Shop online, request a catalog, or explore any one of the 39 Penzeys stores nationwide.

Zingerman's
422 Detroit Street
Ann Arbor, MI 48104
Tel: 888 636 8162
www.zingermans.com
What began in 1982 as small deli with great sandwiches has grown to a global foods paradise. Zingerman's selection of Italian cheeses, estate-bottled olive oils, and varietal vinegars is unmatched. Their website and catalog are packed with information.

The Italian Trade Commission
33 E 67th Street
New York, NY 10065
www.italianmade.com
The US official site of the foods and wines of Italy. Includes how to eat Italian-style, where to eat and buy Italian produce in the US, history, and lore of Italian foods and wines.

index

photography credits

KEY: *bg = background*

All photographs by Martin Brigdale except:

Peter Cassidy
Pages 26, 30, 31, 34, 37*bg*, 42 *inset*, 51*bg*, 55, 64, 71, 76, 81, 82 *inset*, 85, 93 *inset*, 96 *inset*, 97, 106 *inset*, 107, 117 *inset*, 121 *inset*, 141, 156, 157*bg*, 160

Michelle Garrett
Page 17

Jeremy Hopley
Page 5

Richard Jung
Pages 19, 37 *inset*, 38, 41 *inset*, 45, 57, 72 *inset*, 76*bg,* 82*bg*, 94, 100, 104, 105, 106*bg*, 117*bg*, 121*bg*

William Lingwood
Page 114

Jason Lowe
Page 4 *centre & right*
Back cover

David Merewether
Page 109

Diana Miller
Pages 56, 135

David Munns
Page 140

Noel Murphy
Page 51 *inset*

Yuki Sugiura
Pages 147, 153 *inset*

Debi Treloar
Pages 4 *left*, 63 *inset*, endpapers

Ian Wallace
Page 146

Kate Whitaker
Pages 21*bg*, 22, 25, 33, 41*bg*, 42*bg*, 46, 47, 48, 52, 63*bg*, 68*bg*, 72*bg*, 86, 93*bg*, 96*bg*, 99*bg*, 113*bg*, 122, 124, 131*bg*, 136*bg*, 143, 144*bg*, 153*bg*, 158, 159

Clare Winfield
Front cover

Francesca Yorke
Page 75